Entertaining, wi~
approach to care~
book about career c~~~

Sir Ian Davis, Businessman, For~~~ ~~
Director of McKinsey Company and Rolls Royce
Chairman

A Groundhog Career tackles one of the most crucial questions in work and life: how do I find my purpose? The authors provide a comprehensive blueprint for identifying what truly matters on your career and life journey. With insightful guidance and practical advice, this book will help you navigate your path to a fulfilling and meaningful career.

Daniel Obst, President and Chief Executive Officer,
AFS Intercultural Programs

Career advice reimagined for our times. There is great wisdom in this highly entertaining and thought-provoking new take on how to get the most from professional life. I only wish I'd been given this book much earlier in my career as it would have come in handy!

Trisha Conley, Executive Vice President,
People and Culture at LyondellBasell

A transformative guide to help you break free from career traps and find true fulfilment. The modern-day guide to finding your *ikigai*: what you love, what you're good at, what the world needs, and what you can find success in.

A must-read for those contemplating whether and how to reshape their career path.

Jaron Soh, Co-Founder and Chief Executive Officer, VODA, The LGBTQIA+ Mental Health App

If you've ever felt that you were getting exactly what you think you wanted… watch out, it can turn out to be a trap because you might lose yourself in exchange – just as the clever friend of this story's hero remarks right at the beginning.

Drs Schuster & Oxley's newest book doesn't only provide us with a good story – and with advice for a satisfying work life, based on real-life experiences – it also provides readers young and old with 'ingredients of joy'. So don't miss it!

Ulrike Lunacek, Former Vice President of the European Parliament

An insightful and relatable book with practical advice on how to navigate the complexities of career progression and the sometimes-confusing choices that we face on our individual journey. A must-read.

Chan Boodhai, Chief Industry Officer, bp/ Sustainable Market Initiative (SMI)

A gripping story with wonderfully insightful introspection and thought exercises.

Oliver Carter, Online Creator and Founder of Brainy Creators

This book stands out as one of the best and most relatable guides on career advice, particularly for an 18-year-old like me. Shey's story, which illustrates the importance of self-discovery and personal fulfilment while focusing on career advancement, is crafted in a way that every young person can truly connect with, providing essential lessons.

Sebastian Paar, Austrian Student

A Groundhog Career has been a revelation, blending behavioural science with practical wisdom. It reimagines the workplace from a grind into a source of fulfilment and purpose. For anyone navigating modern career complexities, this book is an indispensable guide.

Jendrik Sielaff, German Hockey Athlete and HR Professional

A thought-provoking read that challenges the way we view our jobs, society, and the pervasive influence of technology. This book is not just a casual read; it's a wake-up call that compels readers to reassess perspectives on various aspects of modern professional life. By illustrating the broader implications of our work, the authors push us to think beyond the routine and recognize the deeper significance of our roles. This book is a catalyst for introspection, urging us to question our assumptions and think critically about the societal norms we often take for granted. In addition to its philosophical insights, it's packed with useful tips and tricks.

Nitesh Prakash, Partner at Bain & Company

A beacon for anyone feeling lost in the corporate maze. Schuster and Oxley's *A Groundhog Career* offers a transformative approach to professional life, urging us to break free from the system's confines and rediscover our true selves.

Felix Henderson, Serial Entrepreneur, Co-Founder and Chief Operating Officer of Oh

An inspiring read that captures the fear and liberation of leaving corporate life to follow one's passion. A must-read for aspiring entrepreneurs.

Niharika Prakash, Founder of Moolae

A Groundhog Career oozes class from start to finish. A bucket list must-read for all business professionals – young, budding, aged, tenured, retired. Insightful, magnificent, awesome, fantastic, brilliant, reflective – dare say a perspective changing masterpiece. Just wow!

Ashwani Prashara, Chief HR Officer, O2C, Reliance Industries

Brilliant book that is full of career strengthening, practical advice. Highly recommended for budding entrepreneurs and aspiring professionals who want to make an impact through their actions.

Anand Verma, Green Tech Entrepreneur, Founder and Chief Executive Officer of ExpectAI

A TALE OF CAREER TRAPS
AND HOW TO ESCAPE THEM

A GROUNDHOG CAREER

DR HELMUT SCHUSTER
&
DR DAVID OXLEY

First published in Great Britain by Practical Inspiration Publishing, 2025

© Dr Helmut Schuster and Dr David Oxley, 2025

Book cover and illustrations by Andy 'Doodles' Baker.

The moral rights of the authors have been asserted.

ISBN   9781788607087   (hardback)
       9781788607094   (paperback)
       9781788607117   (epub)
       9781788607100   (mobi)

Want to bulk-buy copies of this book for your team and colleagues? We can customize the content and co-brand *A Groundhog Career* to suit your business's needs.

Please email info@practicalinspiration.com for more details.

Practical Inspiration
Publishing

Dedication

For Sue,
and
For Elfriede.

Table of contents

Introduction

How do we find work that fulfils us? Must we accept that our jobs will always be a burden? Is there anything we can do to improve our professional experience? Indeed, to what extent can we escape the feeling of being a prisoner of our work, and instead, search for a career that not only satisfies us but sustains and invigorates as well?

This book explores these questions. We examine why our motivations and ambitions for work have a profound impact on how we feel about it. We see what we can learn about the root causes of those who find themselves most disillusioned and contrast that with the ingredients for joy. For every example of someone we know who hates their job, there are others that are positively effusive. We ask what's the difference and can we choose one over the other?

Our general disillusionment with work has increased over recent years. In many ways, this is counterintuitive. The world we experience today offers us so many more opportunities and choices. Most of us accept that the general standard of living and quality of life available to us now is much improved from 50 years ago. And yet, the evidence, as we shall see, points to greater levels of dissatisfaction with our professional lives.

We dedicate this book to finding, answering and, more importantly, sharing some ideas on how to change that.

Before we proceed further, let us address and dispel the myth of the most common explanation for high levels of work dissatisfaction: the supposed entitled expectations of Generation Z (Gen Z).[1] Recently, the idea that work should provide more meaning in our lives has received a lot of attention. The UCL professor Anthony Klutz is credited with coining the phrase 'great resignation' to describe the phenomenon of record numbers of people resigning their jobs in 2021 and 2022.[2] Attempts to explain the unprecedented levels included observations that there were generational shifts in regard to expectations about the role work plays in our lives.

Few of us would dispute that our lives have become faster, more hectic, more complicated over the past few decades. It is also fair to say that each generation has different work aspirations. The societal and economic context of 2024 is very different to 1984 and certainly 1954. Obviously, our outlooks and thinking are shaped in powerful ways by that context. In 1954, our parents' expectations about work and what constituted a 'good life' were very different to how we think of them today. Work choices were relatively narrow. In the western economies, there were essentially blue- and white-collar professions. The pinnacle of ambition was to get a job with a big company who 'would look after you' until retirement.

In 1984, the world of work started to benefit from new possibilities. Those of us who entered the workplace in the 80s started to imagine new possibilities, new destinations, both geographically and economically. We still tended to view the world of work as one where companies held most of the power. However, we began to see more choice. We started to imagine new possibilities and nuances for our professional lives. Artificial boundaries and limitations in organizations were eroding. We benefited from the growing consciousness that talent, merit, and capability should matter more than social status, gender, sexual orientation, or ethnicity.

The generation beginning their careers today enter a world transformed by technology and an era of prolonged relative economic prosperity. Their childhoods were shaped by globalization, lowering of class barriers, improvements in access to education, and parents who reframed professional aspiration from purely financial consideration to more altruistic possibilities. This is the first generation educated not just in a traditional classroom, but with real-time access to the cumulative wisdom of humanity's last 3,000 years. When we add to this the now extraordinary spectrum of professional choices available for them, it shouldn't be a surprise that, generally, they have still higher expectations for the role work will play for them.

So, the reasoning goes, Gen Z's lofty expectations for well-paid work that allows them to blur work and personal boundaries while expecting to be absolved from the old organizational conventions of power and access is why we saw such unprecedented levels of job turnover during the COVID-19 pandemic. The trouble is, this might be more generational judgement than fact-based assertion.

Gallup's annual survey that tracks our collective relationship to work has largely stayed consistent over the past 30 years.[3] Around 60% of us find little meaning and take little fulfilment from our work and a staggering 20% say that it is the main reason they feel completely miserable. Another report published last year by UK's leading HR professional body, CIPD, cited as many as 90% of us were disengaged with our jobs.[4] And finally, a report from Pew Research in 2023 shows that there is little reason to suggest that this is solely a Gen Z or Millennial dynamic. Pew found that 50% of Boomers were dissatisfied with their jobs versus 55% for the younger generations.[5]

The evidence we suggest points to a much more pervasive and troubling phenomenon. Many of us have been conditioned to accept a degree of suffering in and sacrifice from work. We inherit this from our parents and grandparents – a deeply ingrained fatalistic outlook that is driven by dogged belief systems. From the Protestant work ethic of the 17th and 18th centuries, through the emergent labour movements of the 19th and 20th centuries, to every generation's well-intended desire to help their children strive for financial security and social respectability, we are taught to approach our careers from a quantitative perspective.

We aim for a well-paid job. We balance effort for reward. We generally relate to employers and business opportunities as things to 'take advantage of'. Implicit is a perspective of carrying a healthy scepticism about the world of work, a distrust for others' intentions, and, perhaps most importantly, a singlemindedness that pushes us to strive for 'the most we can get'. Think about how your parents advised you through your first professional years. The questions you fielded from family and friends. How were those questions shaped? How did they frame success?

This social conditioning is at the very foundation of why work is often a source of unhappiness in our lives. You reap what you sow. As explainable and even understandable as it is, if we look at our careers solely as a transaction then that is all we will get.

We think two things shape the answer to how we judge satisfaction with our careers: (1) the spectrum of opportunities the world offers, and (2) our capacity to imagine ourselves achieving them. We have all moved with the times and shifted our perspectives. Gen Z may be at the leading edge, but Millennials, Gen X, and Boomers, have all adjusted expectations as well. We all expect more from work. We all have much greater choice about what we choose to do as a profession. Logically, therefore, we explain our increasing levels of work disillusionment with a growing consciousness that we have more and more choice. We look around and make conscious and unconscious observations. We see new possibilities and make comparisons between ourselves and others: 'Look at all these new things I could do, others seem to be much happier with their work than I do, and wouldn't it be great if I could do something for a living that made me happy.' Then, we make excuses or dismiss the observations as impractical or unattainable. In the process, the dark cloud that follows us grows a little bigger.

So, what is the secret to finding fulfilment? What do the roughly 50% of us who are content and fulfilled know that the rest of us don't? And how do we join them? Someone should write a book about that...

We make a lot of choices throughout our professional lives. At some point, we all start to wonder if the superficial transaction layer is all there is. This need for some greater purpose is consistent with who we are as human beings. It is encoded in our DNA. Abraham Maslow, the celebrated American psychologist from the 1940s, theorized that we are pre-disposed to improve ourselves.[6] He offered the suggestion of a pyramid of increasingly sophisticated psychological needs. Once we conquer our primordial needs we seek affiliation, love, respect, and self-knowledge. In short, we start to struggle with the question: 'Is this all there is?'

So, let us set out for you how we plan to tackle this challenge. First, we look at what happens when we get stuck in a one-dimensional career world. We explore how relating to work as a zero-sum game, as something to be leveraged and maximized, can lead to some extraordinarily bad outcomes. Paradoxically, this is the path that may lead to levels of financial and material success but moral and spiritual bankruptcy. It ends up becoming a trap, a vicious downward spiral. We have referred to this as finding yourself a prisoner in a gilded cage.

We point out that we don't do this randomly or without encouragement. There are co-conspirators. The world around us makes it complicated for us to separate our own needs from those around us. Society celebrates and pushes ideals of success that are distorted by consumerism, celebrity, status, and privilege. We are also conditioned to please others. In fact, this is one of the most powerful and intoxicating forces that drive us, particularly in our early careers. Who doesn't want to make their parents happy and proud? And then there are our competitive instincts. We are aware that friends and colleagues are competing for something, so we throw ourselves into the game, and we play to win.

As we attempt to bludgeon ahead in the professional world, we can leave some collateral damage. An important aspect of this is created by 'leadership dystopia'. The idea that our goal should be to attain leadership for its status and power. We unpack how this can not only lead us to cause others unnecessary damage but also how it can create perverse consequences for us personally.

Finally, we offer some advice, ideas, lessons, and wisdom. The goal of this book is to help unlock secrets to finding greater levels of fulfilment and meaning in your career. We firmly believe that each of us has the capacity to change our own fate. If you really want to feel more engaged, more fulfilled, more sustained by your career... there is a path for you to do that.

When we wrote our first book *A Career Carol*, it was born from a concern that business, leadership, and specifically career advice books, needed reimagining. This emanated from shared frustrations that existing books seemed indulgent, dense, and academic. We have both enjoyed studying and writing academically, but we would be among the first to admit it can be insular. It can sometimes be tough to read without an Enigma-like decoding device. Moreover, we were particularly conscious of how 'generation now' feels ignored. In our coaching discussions, there was a distinct reluctance to slog through the text of classic and modern volumes to find the one or two nuggets deeply buried within.

The burning need, we felt, was to find a way to convey important, substantial, and relevant subjects in a more accessible, engaging, and practical format.

Judging by the reception *A Career Carol* received, we must have got something right! Our attempts to write something different, something that put storytelling at the heart of the endeavour resonated. We often extract greater wisdom from the best stories we've heard than from books supposedly designed to deliver business advice. Stories amuse, engage, and stimulate our imagination in ways that pure analysis and theories don't. Consequently, we have set out once again in *A Groundhog Career* to stimulate right- and left-brain thinking. To put storytelling at the heart of the book, sharing a colourful and entertaining tale designed to illuminate the consequences and remedies for finding career fulfilment.

In Part I, we tell the story of Shey Sinope as he turns 30 years old. This is the same Shey we introduced you to in our first book. For those of you interested in Shey's journey, this will read as a sequel or continuation of his professional journey. If, however, you are starting your Drs Schuster & Oxley investment with this book, do not worry. The fable will read as a simple stand-alone cautionary tale of the dangers of getting exactly what you think you wanted… only to discover that isn't really what you needed. You will still want to buy the first book though. Trust us on that.

In Part II, we provide an explanation and analysis of the key points. Another feature of our first book that is repeated here are the perspectives and voices from some distinguished contributors. The real stories, lessons, and advice from this impressive multi-generational group is once again a highlight of the book. Part II is designed to appeal to the left-brain thinkers with blink summaries and tools designed to help you think through the issues. We only share tools we have used and found helpful. In some cases, these tools were gifted to us by extraordinarily talented coaches, mentors, colleagues, friends, and teachers. One of their greatest powers was the generosity to share their wisdom without reservation. In writing this book, we hope to again pay some of those lessons forward in a refreshed format, accessible to a new audience.

Finally, before you return or begin your journey with Shey Sinope and Drs Schuster & Oxley, let us address a final question that may be lingering in your minds. On what basis do we share this story and advice? Well, you might look at our educations, our doctoral training, related research, and that might make you comfortable that we have a very good grounding in the behavioural science that underpins the challenges of navigating a fulfilling career. Or you might look at our respective 40-year careers in consulting, Fast-Moving-Consumer-Goods (FMCG), commodity trading, and energy. We worked with some extraordinary leaders in the UK, USA, India, Middle East, and continental Europe. In the process, we like to think we helped those leaders and the businesses they led achieve some impressive results. Much of our work involved optimizing individual and team performance, and, like many professional sports coaches might also observe, the secret to extraordinary performance started with helping individuals become the best version of themselves.

Perhaps one of these explanations provides you with sufficient reassurance your time investment will be well made. However, we have entered this writing collaboration with a purpose and goal that is a bit different than simply pointing to our past training and experiences. After all, while the past teaches us many lessons, it is important we live in the now, deal with what's before us, and embrace the constantly changing context. So, our aim with this book is to be more of a mentor or coach. Your personal thought partner or sounding board. The big distinction with this book is to think about things that are difficult to talk about. Things that we, over the years, have been conditioned to believe we must either ignore or deny. The doubts and insecurities we can't be open about with society, community, family, friends, and work colleagues for fear of harsh judgement.

So, our goal is to create a safe space for us to discuss questions that may be difficult for you to find another outlet to work through. And, therefore, while it may sound strange, we think the main criterion for investing your time in this book, is that we might be surprisingly good listeners. A book, with words, that you read, but in the process, find time, space, encouragement, permission, practical tools, to say things, admit things, experiment with thoughts, that you otherwise might avoid.

However, failing all of that... we think the next chapter in the Shey Sinope saga is an entertaining tale that will give you a handsome return for a few hours' investment. As we have mentioned before, our criterion for success in our writing is to produce something that is (whimsically) entertaining, and in the process, help at least one person become a better version of themselves. We hope that person is you.

PART I

A GROUNDHOG CAREER

Chapter 1

There was a storm brewing

Shey Sinope looked out of the window of his apartment. From the 20th floor, he could see the downtown skyscrapers, like giant silver tombstones framed against the fast-setting sun. In the background, a verse from one of his favourite bands played. The song by *James* spoke to Shey's mood. The idea of finding yourself ridiculous and inviting others to join you. He thought the lyrics were clever and appealed for some reason… he wasn't quite sure why.

'Two steps forward and one back?' he asked himself. He was introspecting. One of the things he'd learned through the difficult transition from college to professional life was to occasionally take stock on where he was. Life was hectic and he knew he preferred to be a passenger sometimes. Carried by waves of circumstance and others' expectations. It was simply easier than the alternative.

'Swimming against a strong current?' *Is that closer to how I feel?* Introspection was hard. Like trying to name vague, almost fleeting, emotions and feelings. He felt he was missing something. Something elusive. After all, he should be feeling quite content. Happy even. Five years ago, he was euphoric at landing the job at MGL Mania

Intelligence. One of the premier AI firms in the world. He surprised himself at how quickly he learned the internal game of career ladders. He remembered excitedly sharing his discover with his friend Ellen Elpis.

෪ඏ

'And would you believe this button here transmits an emergency signal and provides a homing beacon for international rescue teams.' Shey showed Ellen his new Swiss watch. 'It's super cool, isn't it?'

'Well, yes, it does look… expensive. But how likely is it that you will need to trigger an international SOS on your commute from mid-town to downtown?' Ellen asked.

Ignoring her, Shey continued, 'And did I tell you about flying Emirates first class? Not only do you get a personal cabin, but you also have your own shower at 35,000 feet! Crazy cool.'

'You do seem very enamoured by it all. But what about the work itself? Do you enjoy that?' Ellen continued, trying to move the conversation along.

'Oh, yes. That's fine. I've moved on from coding to managing projects. See, that's what matters. You have to figure out how the game is played. Not the "work" or the "product", certainly not "the customer". The internal career game is all about figuring out how to maximize your personal return. Build your internal career capital. You do that by figuring out what the key leadership movers and shakers "think" is important. Once I figured out that formula, I never looked back. You want to know what it is? The secret sauce of climbing the corporate ladder?' Shey barely paused for Ellen to open her mouth. He grabbed a napkin and scribbled an equation:

$$\frac{VE \ (\textbf{Visible Effort}) + TI \ (\textbf{Targeted Insights}) + SN \ (\textbf{Smart Networking}) + DH \ (\textbf{Disarming Humor})}{UCB \ (\textbf{Unchecked boxes})}$$

'Brilliant, isn't it?' Shey beamed. 'Ever since I've started using this equation, I've seen a massive uptick in my fortunes. It's a simple scale that I track weekly. The higher the overall number, the faster my career velocity. I started in single digits, but now I'm consistently above 100! Three promotions in the last two years! It's a lot of work so you have to be really careful to focus for maximum impact. After all, what's the point of putting effort in if it doesn't advance your personal goals? That's the fundamental point, isn't it? Too many people simply do what they are told and expect some sort of leap of faith recognition. I call BS on that. I'm only interested in expending energy where I know it's going to get me what I want. Promotions, pay raises, bonuses.'

'The foundational principle is visible effort,' Shey continued. 'You put the hours in when you know the right people will see it. It's not as simple as leaving your suit jacket on the back of the chair overnight or leaving your car in the parking lot and Uber-ing home. Those things don't really work. No, the best approach is to pick a workstation close to key leaders. Be there when they come in and as they leave at night. In between, you find ways to "help out" on whatever they think is urgent on any given day. It doesn't really matter what it is. Work from home has made this more complicated but I have found workarounds. You just have to make sure you know what your key management contacts are up to... where they are on any given day... then plan your activities around that.

'Then I work on targeted insights. I prepare carefully for town halls and meetings with senior leaders to understand their likes/dislikes and red buttons. I make sure I am one of the first to ask them a question that simultaneously makes them look good, while eliciting a "good question" response. I rank my performance based on the number of "good question" virtual back-pats I get per week. My record is 20!

'Smart networking is my superpower. I've made a map of the key leaders in my part of the business. It's easy enough with all the org charts available. I then rank them based on my calculation of their influence in the organization. That's also easy to figure out based on what other leaders say about them.

'Humour is also an essential ingredient. Timing can be the only tricky part. However, I find that not only is it something I have a natural flair for, but also it's incredibly effective at defusing awkward moments. You know I discovered sarcasm in my teens. I've now expanded my repertoire and mainly prefer abstract irreverence. The main benefit is that it avoids any risk of inadvertent personal offence. I use it most to sidestep awkwardness and change the course of conversations I think may be getting away from me. I like to think I win people over with it as well. After all, laugh and the whole world laughs with you.

'Then, the only other thing is checking the annoying compliance boxes. You know all the administrative stuff that HR and other support departments think are important. It's just like taking your vaccinations. It's mainly BS, but it's the price of playing the game, like the entry fee. So, you just check the boxes as quickly and painlessly as you can. I divide my score by anything that I haven't got to within 48 hours. It can really kill your score if you're not careful.

'It's brilliant... fool proof... I am a genius!'

A silence fell over the coffee shop table. Shey was expecting something like awed reverence from Ellen. Instead, the pause grew to an unbearable length... 10 seconds... 15 seconds.

'Shey... you want me to be impressed. To confirm for you how clever you are. Well, I don't think anyone has ever doubted your IQ, least of all me. You are undoubtedly one of the smartest people I've ever met. And yet, I wonder if you have also lost yourself in all of this. So, let me ask you just one question… are you happy?' Ellen asked.

'Well… DUH… OF COURSE I AM! I've not just managed to launch my career, but I'm travelling at warp speed. I'm making fantastic money. My employer loves me. And wait for it, my parents think I'm some captain of industry! I've never received this sort of adulation from my family,' Shey answered theatrically.

༄ༀ

Shey knew he had overdone things with Ellen. What had started as a routine catch-up over coffee had somehow morphed into him showing off. He could be a bit of an asshole. Shey's friendship with Ellen was as close as any he had in his life. Who was he kidding? It was the only real friendship he had. He was relieved when a week later Ellen had called and asked if he could help her with introductions at MGL Mania Intelligence. She was looking to raise some funds or get some pro bono help for her community activist alliance (non-government organization (NGO)). She wanted to pitch MGL Mania Intelligence the idea of a community service algorithm that encouraged and rewarded good deeds. Shey saw the opportunity to ease his conscience. He paused his formula for a day and pushed to get Ellen connected to the right people.

What does being happy have to do with it? Careers are about money, status, influence, respect, access to people in a position to bestow more, Shey told himself.

Ellen's question had lingered. It was now dark outside. The downtown skyscrapers were impressively illuminated. The city view demonstrating to him how wonderful objects can appear when they are cleverly designed and ingeniously lit.

Careers are a foot race to the top. But it's more like Squid Games than the Olympics. Shey thought about a few of his contemporaries at work. Generally, he dismissed them all as irrelevant, as background noise. Except… Emi Silva. Shey shivered. Saying his name left a nasty taste. *Emi without doubt is proof that all is fair in love, war, and plotting to bury your rivals at work!*

Increasingly, Shey found himself pitched against Emi at work. Not in a getting-work-done sense, more in an effort to curry favour and gain the undisputed title of 'most likely to be the next senior executive'. Every time Shey won a battle, gained an accolade, so did Emi. Shey had come to loathe Emi. He had become something of a caricature in Shey's mind. Where Shey had an ordered scientific approach, Emi was erratic, unpredictable, emotional. While there were many things about Emi that grated, it was his scattered divergent thinking that Shey hated most. Honestly, why take a problem and expand it to a universe of variables when that just made things harder?

How the leaders at work saw anything in Emi, other than a walking reminder of chaos theory, was beyond Shey. Whenever Shey saw Emi, he pictured imaginary bubble quotes above his head: *'Do I really look like someone with a plan? You know what I am? I'm a dog chasing cars. I wouldn't know what to do with one if I caught it! You know, I just… DO things.'*

Shey had just turned 30. A milestone he didn't choose to celebrate, other than the obligatory family gathering. Just another year. Nothing noteworthy. He was fully focused on pushing his career as far and as fast as he could. Beating the competition. He dreamed of one day being declared victor in his private rivalry with Emi. It meant long hours. It meant making sacrifices. That was quite easy actually because his life really involved little more than work.

Tomorrow he was due to attend the final day of a career accelerator programme being held at the offices of some industrial psychologist consultants. Two weeks earlier he had received an email from his employer's HR department. It had sounded euphoric, giddy almost. 'We are delighted to inform you that you have been nominated to attend our accelerated leadership programme. Congrats!' He'd had a virtual meeting with the Head of HR the previous week.

'Chey Sinobe?' Ralph Canine the Chief HR Officer shouted down the phone, pronouncing his name wrong with an emphasis on an imagined 'ch'.

'This is… Shey.'

'Congrats on being nominated for our career acceleration programme. We call it "CAPs." We give everyone a personalized company baseball hat on the final day. People seem to love the hats.' Ralph, after years in HR, may have found the toll eating away at his perceptions of reality. 'Anyhow, I wanted to call and wish you well. I have high hopes for you, Chey. I've been doing this job now for many years, and your nomination was the first time that every single member of the nomination committee agreed. Normally, we get a nomination with two or three sponsors. In your case all ten members of the committee seemed to know you and were keen for you to be a part of the programme. In fact, you and one other colleague have set some new benchmarks this year. Impressive effort… you've clearly been busy!'

Shey knew exactly who was on the committee and had spent the last three months doing his groundwork. It had been reasonably easy to find out who the committee members were. Four were in his direct work sphere and so he was confident that each of them would be supporters. He managed to find out who the other six were by simply asking open questions, letting his colleagues volunteer the information. Then he slowly chipped away to make sure he had met with and done some work with all of them. The modern invention of boundaryless organizations and informal agile teams really helped. Sure, to achieve his goal, he had to pretend to be interested in everything from the nutritional value of cafeteria food to the carbon footprint of the office campus. But he understood that these projects were not important other than the access they allowed him to critical decision makers. All part of the proven career success formula. And it worked.

Of course, he knew Ralph's not-so-cryptic comment meant that Emi must also have made it onto the programme. Shey knew it was likely. He seemed to mesmerize people with his whirlwind of waving arms and passionate nonsense. Classic case of camouflaging a vacuum by saying it with animated conviction. Shey reflected that if he ever started a company to sell snow in the Antarctic, Emi should be the lead negotiator.

ঔৱেঞ্জ

The first two days of the career accelerator had been predictable. The programme participants had attended separately. It seemed they were reserving group interaction for some final flourish. On the first day, Shey sat through a battery of psychometric tests. The Wonderlic, the FIBRO B, Myers Briggs, Dimensions, and a few others. Shey had researched them all. He was mildly fascinated by how a test for the compatibility of submariners would apply to a contemporary corporate setting. If they were ever in a Noah-like flood, he imagined it might be useful.

Most of this work was easy to predict, prepare for, and generally didn't cause too many troubles. You could take prep tests in advance. If you simply approached them like a Graduate Management Admission Test (GMAT), you couldn't go too far wrong. Oh, but never forget the golden rule… no matter what anyone says… remember everything counts and everything is a test.

The second day was about company stuff. All the current 'strategy and culture' jargon. Shey knew what the company's leadership were most worried about. It was strange that the rhetoric wasn't as easy for most people to pick up on. It was like feeling a metaphorical strong breeze. The words, tone, body language. It all pointed toward some very clear agenda. Costs are a problem, people! Let's control costs! Or we need to centralize… there are too many pet projects distracting us… centralize and consolidate… focus people! The current theme was creativity, innovation, and encouraging entrepreneurship. Of course, this meant less central control, more degrees of freedom, a little less efficient, but hey, we will conveniently forget that we are here because of the whole eliminate-degrees-of-freedom initiatives of a couple of years ago. He remembered the recent meeting with one executive who extolled the virtues of going backwards and forwards at the same time. Of course, this made little sense, but you learn to accept that it's less about making sense and more about demonstrating alignment. The answer was, generally, just to mimic. It's quality, price, and speed, people… all three… no compromises!

Shey was confident he had done well so far, and he had just the final day to navigate. He was a little nervous because the final day was more of a black box. Try as he might, it had been tremendously hard to get intelligence on what was involved. All he got were platitudes like, 'Just be yourself' or 'The key is to be completely genuine; they can smell a fake a mile away.' What he did know was that the psychologists were being paid to find reasons, failings, faults with everyone on the course. This made him feel anxious. He was very confident that this last day, and perhaps a showdown with Emi, were all that remained between him and the promise of a company sponsored accelerated executive placement. It was well known that this was how MGL Mania Intelligence grew their next generation of C-suite occupants. And how cool and crazy would that be? Shey Sinope, the indecisive, deeply insecure, introverted, near recluse, on the verge of being anointed a senior executive at a *FORTUNE 500* company!

Shey had come a long way from his college student incarnation seven years earlier. He still remembered vividly the night before his graduation ceremony. He vowed he would never let himself slide back into that sea of despondency and helplessness. Back then, he had a little help breaking free of his self-imposed inertia. He prided himself on how he had taken those lessons and built a kick-ass career for himself. Conquering his career had become his crusade. It was a source of extraordinary pride to Shey that what he had originally feared was well behind him. The challenge to get a good job, and become a virtuoso at playing the corporate game, ended up being much easier, more intuitive, than he ever expected. He loved being good at it. More than that, he was in love with the sense of identity, power, and purpose it gave him.

I'm not good at much of anything else, but this corporate ladder business... I'm a black belt. He thought about this late at night. It was his affirmation. It made him feel good.

In that moment, he remembered his family birthday party and the strange story that his uncle had told him.

৩০৫৪

'... happy birthday to you!' sang the small gathering. Shey obligingly blew out the 30 candles.

'I can't tell you what I wished for, Mum.' He antici- pated and headed off the next question.

'OK... but tell me this... was it for a beautiful stranger to come into your life and give your parents grandbabies?'

'I knew it was too good to be true. Nearly 90 minutes and I was beginning to think I'd actually survive a family gathering without the emotional ambush. Fortunately, we live in a world and a society where I don't have to live for my parents' dreams.'

'Let him be, little sis,' said Uncle Freddy. He could normally be relied upon to defuse and dismantle these emotional unexploded bombs. One of the benefits of having a, now retired, psychology professor as a close relative and Godfather. 'You know he's too in love with himself to have a healthy relationship with another human being… until we can master cloning that is.'

'Wow… it is my birthday, Uncle. Cut me some slack!' Shey didn't mind the ribbing too much. He knew his uncle had his back.

Shey's parents busied themselves with cake cutting and taking orders from the half dozen guests.

'So, how are things really, Shey? I know you've been working hard, prioritizing your career, but how do you feel about it… really?' asked Uncle Freddy.

'I'm amazed at how good I am at this career thing. That still feels novel to me. But given where I was in college, it's still a big step forward for me. I don't feel unfulfilled. Quite the contrary, I feel like I'm practising for my version of the Olympics. I don't yet know how fast or far I can go. It just makes sense to test those limits, doesn't it?'

Uncle Freddy nodded. 'OK. And other than work, what else are you spending time on?'

'Nothing really. I try to get to the gym a couple of times a week. But, even then, I use the time to think through work-related problems or opportunities.'

'And the work, does the work itself feel important?'

'In the sense that I think I've decoded what people really value… and I do like the recognition and positive feedback,' Shey responded.

'And what about the people at work? Do you have any close friendships?'

'Acquaintances is probably the right word. I don't see the point in putting down roots with the people at work. It's all so transitory. We change project teams every few months and people go in different directions. I also plan to be their boss, so friendships might complicate that.'

'Interesting. But you feel OK? Are you sleeping OK? No strange dreams or ghostly visitations?'

'Oh… no… fortunately. No ghostly commencement speakers or anything like that. I generally can't remember my dreams.'

'OK. So Shey, before you are called back to eat some cake, let me tell you a very quick story. I'd like you to reflect on it. You're still doing the weekly introspections?'

Shey nodded.

'If you see no meaning in it, discard it. If, however, it provides you with comfort and insight, use it.' Uncle Freddy smiled. 'Some years ago, I invited some of my former students to my home to hear about how they were doing. Around a dozen visited that evening. Several worked in banking, some in consulting, and a couple had built their own technology firms. They all told me how amazing they were doing. They inferred they had all made lots of money, lived in lovely homes, travelled to exotic places. I told them it was tradition for me on these occasions to serve them all coffee. I diligently made the best coffee I could. As you know, it's not just the beans and the grind, the water is an often-overlooked ingredient. I carefully selected a dozen assorted cups and mugs. Different sizes, some new, some old, some plain, some decorated with colourful patterns. When I returned, I asked them to help themselves. I watched carefully as they jockeyed to get the shiniest and best-looking cups. There was some discussion about the cups and even a bit of bragging by those who felt they had nabbed the best ones. I waited for a quell in conversation as they began sipping the coffee. Then I said, "How many of you are aware or conscious of the value you placed on your cups? Since they are all equally capable of delivering my excellent coffee to your mouths, and do not alter its taste at all, it is interesting that you should all have placed such importance on them. Let me ask you all, do you view your worlds, your lives, your personal identities, by the cups you drink from or the quality of their contents?'"

'Uncle Freddy has always been very cryptic. And anyway, coffee does taste better out of a nice cup!' Shey found himself talking to the skyscraper view again. *I don't think I'm missing anything,* he thought. *Anyway, introspection is what you do when you think you might need a course correction. I'm on a roll. I've built some momentum. I've invested a lot of hard work to get this far. This is not the time for doubt or indecisiveness. I'm going to close this down. Crush any lingering, elusive, feelings of… absence… vacuum. That's just the anxiety of the big day tomorrow playing tricks on me.*

His phone alarm binged. 'Thank God for that. Always the longest 30 minutes of my week! Time to get some rest before the big day.' He refocused his eyes and looked at his reflection in the glass. 'You are the man, be the ball, strap dynamite to the groundhogs, it's all in the hips, visualize success, see it, manifest it… let's go Charlie Brown!' and with that Shey turned off his music and went to bed.

Chapter 2

Into the breach

'♪♬♬♪♪♬♬♪♬♬'

Shey's phone alarm played his preferred 'Uplift' wake-up tune. Shey reached sleepily for his bedside table. He turned off the alarm. He then picked up his watch. Yes, he could see the time on his phone, but gazing at the elegant object lifted his spirits. The exquisite fusion of analogue and digital was the epitome of sophistication; it was the single most beautiful thing he owned. It whispered in a sultry, sexy voice, *Shey... my darling... it is... 6am, Thursday, June 1st.*

'Two hours to *showtime!*' A little dramatic pizzazz was justified. He had occasionally thought of work as a form of performance art. There was always some drama at work but what he meant was more the sense he had constructed for himself a character, a role, a way of appearing. A sort of method acting approach to achieving professional success.

Shey caught up on news from his various feeds. Important to understand what was going on and the consensus on what was good or bad. Interest rates were up, markets were down, rumours of some regional banks in trouble, fast-moving hurricane, no end to the unrest in eastern Europe.

Shey had a few trusted sources that he would follow each morning. Why take the time to form an opinion when there were so many readily available to try on and see if they fit, off-the-peg analysis. Joe Pagan, the hugely popular podcaster and Tik-Tok celebrity, was always funny and incredibly clever at distilling things. Basically, Joe was saying markets needed a correction to weed out the weaklings, the strong companies would benefit, which would mean better, leaner companies in the medium term. The hurricane was going to disintegrate, high-level windshear would cut its legs away. And eastern Europe, well Joe's view was it continued to be a humanitarian disaster but resulted in some unfriendly rivals being distracted.

'Buzz-buzz… buzz-buzz…' The screen on his phone showed Ellen's name. *No time for idle chatter this morning,* he thought and dismissed the call. *I'll update her when I have some good news to share.*

Shey got ready for his big day. Teeth cleaned, groomed, showered, moisturized, and odour anonymized. He put on his corporate warrior uniform. It was partially about protocols and image, but it also mattered to Shey how he felt. He had found a way to own a smart business casual look that had some little touches. His cufflinks for example… they were flamboyantly Dickensian. His shoes were a dark blue suede that looked like corporate black… but weren't. His socks had a splash of completely unnecessary and random colour completely invisible to most of the world. Some of this was his little way to strike at conformity but he also got a kick out of having these inside jokes… with himself.

An hour later, he neared the end of his commute. A short subway ride, a stop for what Uncle Freddy would call fufu, or bougie, coffee. Hopefully there would be no signs to suggest that the day ahead wouldn't go to plan.

'Iced, no whip, non-sugar vanilla, four shot, oak milk, café latte, with hemp extract and turmeric, for... Sashay... Oooh... nice! Will... SASHAY, please collect their coffee and by all means... Shantay, if you may!' the overly caffeinated amateur comedian-come-Barista yelled across the shop. Shey did occasionally watch the RuPaul show so was familiar with the reference. While his favoured drink was quite specific, you'd be amazed how many similar orders were made each morning.

'SASHAY... the spotlight awaits!' the Barista was enjoying this. Shey suddenly had a sinking feeling in his stomach. *I'm Sashay, aren't I?* he thought. He considered his options. Abort? That seemed the most sensible approach. Get out of there without drawing any attention. Shey quietly slipped out of the side door and headed over to the assessment centre offices. He snuck a glance as the door to the coffee shop swung closed and saw a glimpse of the Barista looking his way. Did they wink at him?

&OCB

A few minutes later Shey approached the reception desk at *FAB Advisory,* the assessment centre's office. The office was in a very fashionable, Soho-like part of town. The street was cobblestoned and the building itself must have been a warehouse at some point. Lots of exposed brick and ironwork.

He took his temporary visitor's badge and followed his guide to the big conference area on the second floor. He was told the day would begin once 'the others' arrived.

'Wait, did you say "others"?' he asked his guide. He looked around to see if he could see Emi.

'Yes, Mr Sinope. Today is the group assessment conclusion. We always run the final day as a collective,' said Julia Hess PhD, Rhodes scholar, and noted TEDx speaker on the dangers of making rash and demeaning assumptions about people you don't know. 'I promise it won't be long. You are the first to arrive. Please help yourself to coffee.'

Shey poured some coffee and sat down to regroup. *This is OK,* he thought. *I know the assessment guys are looking to show they've been tough and exacting. Based on what I hear, about 50% of previous classes have made it through. At the end of the day, FAB need to show rigour. They will need at least a couple of sacrifices. I can maybe help them identify the weakest on the savanna... maybe nudge them to the edge of the herd. Would be great if one of those was Emi... presuming he's here.*

Over the next ten minutes four others arrived. Shey was surprised to learn he didn't know them. Fahad and August arrived first. They worked in support functions, accounting, and finance. Shey hadn't spent much time networking in what he saw as non-core business areas so he wasn't too surprised he couldn't place their names. They were followed by Kieran and Daisy. They worked in operations and customer support. Shey was more familiar with these departments. *This is a good thing,* Shey thought. *These guys don't seem like serious contenders.*

One, I would have heard of them if they were, and two, they are all from the less 'sexy' parts of the organization.

'Boa noite… ola… HELLO!' Emi burst into the room, like a red Portuguese flare thrown by a rowdy football crowd. 'Yes, I am Emi.' He didn't so much walk around the room as cartwheel. He kissed and hugged his introductions. 'Parabéns, meus amigos… PARABÉNS!'

Shey watched as the room contorted towards Emi. It was as if his personality consumed most of the oxygen in the room, dragging everyone towards him.

Emi caught Shey's eye.

'Ah… Shey… we meet again! You are pleased to see me!' Emi understood sarcasm.

'Emi,' Shey responded. 'I sincerely hope you get everything you deserve today.'

'Welcome, everyone!' Bob Challack, the general partner of *FAB Advisory,* seemed a convivial, if rather professorial host. 'It is my pleasure to be your guide through this final day of the career advancement programme for MGL Mania Intelligence. If the last couple of days have proven anything, it is that you are all extraordinarily qualified to be here. It has been our honour to spend time with you all individually. Quite instructive, educational, illuminating.'

He's talking in code, Shey thought. *A rough translation might be – some of you boneheads have amused us greatly with some of your imbecilic answers to our tests.*

'Many of you may be meeting for the first time today. You are, of course, all bound by your shared MGL Mania Intelligence connection. That does mean you all share knowledge and understanding of the company's way of working. However, today you will be working much more closely together. Consequently, it may be helpful to learn a little more about one another before we proceed,' Bob said. 'So, let's start with an icebreaker exercise… have you played two truths and a lie before?'

ಬಂಡ

'… and this is how I came to rescue the elephant that was trapped in the watering hole,' explained Kieran. Most people had assumed that was his lie.

Shey was only paying partial attention. Twenty minutes of his life had been lost to this exercise. Twenty minutes he could have been doing something more useful, like going to the dentist, or writing a strongly worded complaint letter to the coffee shop owner about the unnecessary theatrics their baristas got up to. He was also rehearsing his three personal factoids. The game was a familiar one. You 'won' by using the exercise to humble brag. It was always better to go towards the end of the exercise to size up the other stories and measure your own for optimum impact. Shey knew he had this one in the bag. No question, this was his first win of the day. Kieran finally finished and everyone politely turned to Shey.

'So, how do I follow that, Kieran?' Shey said. 'My three factoids are far less interesting I'm afraid. First, I came up with our company's current tag line "*ensuring the singularity always puts 'U' and 'I' at its heart.*" Second, I have met the famous actor who played *Ether* in those great evil AI movies, and I even rehearsed dialogue with her. And third, I built a trashcan robot as a college senior that came second in an intra-university inventor's competition.'

Shey felt the desired stunned awe at the first claim. He explained he was on the team who had worked with a PR firm to come up with the phrase now emblazoned around their company's offices. Shey had repeated the phrase loudly in a meeting and some present thought he had invented it. He showed a picture on his phone of his trashcan robot design with him holding a #2 rosette. And finally, he explained he had not actually met the actress who played *Ether*. He shared a carefully edited story about how he had an amazingly lifelike dream about meeting her, the night before his graduation.

Shey Sinope 1... everyone else 0.

'I've never understood that. The whole "U" and "I" *sing*. "U" is in the middle of the word but the letter "I" isn't. *Exquisite* makes more sense. Or maybe *Disequilibrium*. *Relinquishment,* even. Hey, everyone, let's see what other words we know that have "UI" in them?' Emi interrupted Shey's mental microphone drop.

Shey wasn't completely shocked at Emi's response. This is what he did. Take something and run off into left field, jabbering meaninglessly. What stunned Shey was the response Emi got. The room suddenly started shouting out words with 'UI' in them.

'Discontinuity!'
'Distinguished!'
'Equivalence!'
'Relinquish!'
'Extinguisher!'
'Ventriloquist!'

The room reached a crescendo of laughter as it embraced the Emi-inspired lateral madness then paused to take breath.

'Well done everyone. I hope you enjoyed finding a little more out about one another. And, Emi, a special thanks to you for that fun word-play game at the end there. A great way for everyone to participate.' As Bob spoke, Shey seethed.

Were these guys really fooled by that? Surely these psychologists humoured while secretly noting the obvious insanity. Shey knew he had nailed that game but now he wasn't sure whether the facts had been obscured by Emi's antics.

෮ᏮᏟᏰ

'Now, let's set up our first role play.' Bob beckoned the group over toward a door. 'We take some pride in making these simulations as realistic as possible. Behind this door we have constructed an environment to add an extra dimension.' Bob opened the door to reveal a half-built igloo in the middle of a snowscape. A freezing wind caught them all by surprise.

Bob handed them each a piece of paper.

'Here are your personal instructions. When you enter the room, you must embrace these instructions. If you deviate from them, it will negatively factor into your performance appraisal. Your goal, as a team, is to survive the night. For today's purposes, that will be 90 minutes. You must do so using the contents of the room and your own ingenuity. To make this as real as possible, we are able to reduce the temperature in the room. After 30 minutes you will find it uncomfortable, 60 minutes most of you will lose dexterity and function of your extremities. Suffice to say, you will want to find shelter from the storm as quickly as possible. We will observe how you tackle this task via the video cameras. Good luck.'

Shey's note read: 'You are physically able, except you have lost the ability to verbally communicate (in any way).'

I know this game. Simple. This is the classic 'parts of the elephant challenge'. It's a great showcase for my secret formula. Cameras and surveillance. Show my initiative and the mime class I took in college drama!

A few minutes later, the six colleagues found themselves in the chilly room. Shey had to admit that it was a convincingly staged simulation. There was fake snow falling from the ceiling with about a foot on the ground. It was Styrofoam or something similar. The partially constructed igloo was made of white plastic bricks. However, the real illusion was how the walls were all painted to give the impression of a frozen tundra for miles around. Once the door was shut you really didn't have to have too much imagination to believe you were six, smart-business-casually dressed, want-to-be executives, stranded in Antarctica.

Shey flew into immediate action. First, he scoped the room to see if he could locate the cameras. He counted four. Shey looked around at the others in the room. He noticed Fahad and August right beneath a camera. He rushed over. Waved his hands to get their attention. Then he hammed-up a classic 'Marcel Marceau at a plate glass window', got slightly carried away with a 'walking against the wind', before regaining his composure and executing the universally understood signal for being unable to speak.

'So,' said Fahad, attempting to ignore Shey, 'I have the ability to talk but not see.'

'… it's strange because that's also what mine said. I am blind. Brought on by the whiteout conditions,' responded August.

Rats, thought Shey. I'd forgotten that aspect of the game. That must mean one of the others is the key to allowing us to communicate. Shey watched as the other three were huddling in the centre of the room. The problem was that they really weren't well placed for any of the camera angles. Shey rushed over to them, waved for their attention, then attempted his best 'dog pulling mime artist on a leash'. When that didn't work, he tried an inventive take on 'there is trouble you must come quick.'

'I think he wants us to follow him,' said Kieran. 'Shey, just so you know, I am unable to move as I have frostbite in my feet. Daisy has frostbite in her hands, and Emi has a concussion and is unconscious. We understand he was the group leader until his accident.'

Shey took stock. *Amazing,* he thought! *This couldn't be more perfect. I know what must happen here. I have to bring Fahad and August over to join Kieran, Emi, and Daisy. I can explain what I know to Kieran and Emi, and they can verbalize it to Fahad and August, who, along with me have no physical constraints on finding and completing the shelter.* Shey then reflected on how best to do this. How best to perform. *So, the goals here must be (1) to show how well I worked to solve the problem, (2) that the group succeeds in the challenge and, maybe, (3) throw those watching some clues on who the weakest links were,* Shey thought. *Is that too calculating, too callous? Well, it's a simulation so no one gets hurt, and it's also a competition, sort of like 'Survivor', the reality TV show.*

Shey tried to capitalize on Emi's incapacity. While he worked toward the simulation's goal, he also attempted to give those observing the impression that Emi was not completely unconscious, and something of an obstacle to the group. A couple of times he did his best 'tripped by an unexpected hazard mime', threw in the 'someone said something unexpected', and in a late flourish, and as some payback for the word alliteration, pretended to work Emi as a ventriloquist's dummy.

Eighty-nine minutes later, Shey and his colleagues emerged from the simulation room. The igloo had been constructed. They all sheltered inside. Bob signalled they had completed their task just within the time limit. The room lights were dimmed, the AC was adjusted, and the door was opened.

'You guys left it late. But you survived,' Bob said. 'It certainly looked like there was a lot of effort going on in there. At one stage, we didn't think you were going to pull that out but those last ten minutes everything came together for you. Shey, you seemed to carry a lot of the load today. The mimed directions for building the shelter were some of the more imaginative and entertaining we've ever seen… well done.'

Shey Sinope 2… everyone else 0.

୫୬୯

Shey couldn't help congratulating himself. He was now clearly ahead. He'd also managed to score against Emi. The Antarctic simulation had worked out beautifully. He had balanced the need to finish with the opportunity to prolong and amplify his role as linchpin. In retrospect, the mute role with knowledge of the shelter plan was perfect. It would have been difficult to achieve the same outcome from one of the other roles. Sometimes he had to admit, luck was a piece of the equation.

After a break for lunch, during which Shey took the opportunity for some alone time, they were greeted again by Bob Challack.

'Everyone, I hope you had a pleasant lunch. It is now time for our second exercise. I will be breaking you up into two groups of three. We call this exercise *The Story*. In your groups, we will ask you to write a short story, 250 words or a page of A4. You will write this story by alternating between each of you as authors, one sentence at a time. You will note, this will be old school, there is a single sheet of lined paper and one pencil. The quality of your stories will be viewed through the following criteria: (1) Is it a complete story with beginning middle and end? (2) Is it coherent with no big jumps? (3) Does it convey something meaningful?

'A couple of important ground rules: Once we call your team names, you may not communicate in any way, other than through your story. Once a sentence is written and your team member has passed it on, it should not be edited. Oh, and one more thing. Just to add a small but interesting twist to this exercise, we will give each of you a random word that you must include in the story. Please capitalize your random word when you use it. You will see we have arranged round tables that rotate to allow you each to take turns. Good luck… now off you go.'

The main point from my perspective, thought Shey, *is that this is a group deliverable. It's hard to separate out the contributions. I wonder if I can find a promotional angle.*

Shey was paired with August and Daisy. They were told to go in alphabetical order. August began. She scribbled away, then passed the paper to Daisy. She began to write and a few seconds later, passed the story to Shey.

You would think it difficult to write a story that explained how a SAUCEPAN came to save the world. And yet, let us explain how that seemingly innocent object when paired with an APRICOT, achieved such a feat.

Shey stared at the paper. He felt a chill down his spine. What were these two playing at? Was this a hospital pass… a set-up? It didn't make sense to sabotage a team exercise. Maybe they realized he was way ahead on the day's scorecard and were just jealous? Then it came to him… a brilliant angle! Thinking fast on his feet, he wrote a 212-word sentence that explained how a great Chef came to prepare an apricot dessert for a hungry tyrant, who after experiencing such mind-altering flavours, changed their ways to become a benevolent and ultimately beloved ruler of the faraway world of PYJAMA Kingdom. *Classic fable subtext about making the best of the circumstances. I can also play this in multiple ways, stretch it into a metaphor on teamwork, sprinkle a little Sinek pixy dust about leaders eating last, and bing-bang-bosh,* thought Shey rather smugly.[1]

Shey Sinope 3… everyone else 0.

৪০৫৪

'Everyone, please join me for our last exercise of the day.' Bob beckoned them into a conference room with a circular seating arrangement. There was a single, black leather seat in the middle of the room. A bright spotlight shone on the seat.

'Please take any seat in the front row,' Bob said. 'Thanks. Now for the final exercise of the day. What we call *Ask Me Anything*. Each of you will be invited to take the hot seat for ten minutes… the QUESTIONED. Your colleagues… THE QUESTIONERS… those who have experienced today with you, will then take turns in asking you any questions they are curious about. The questioned may answer these in any form they wish, including choosing not to. At the end of each session, my team and I *may* ask the questioners about our observations of the questioned. We will only do this if we think there is something interesting to discuss. Again, they can choose to answer however they wish. All clear? Let's proceed.'

A twist? thought Shey. *While I feel nervous about being questioned, at the end of the day, there will be some who feel I may have run over them a bit today. That may result in some tough questions. However, it's also an opportunity for me to use my targeted insights. At worst, this should be a draw. The key is not to be defensive, not to get intimidated, but to stay confident and keep calm.* Shey took some deep breaths, calmed himself. This felt like the final 100 metres of a gruelling marathon where he had put in the hard training – studied relentlessly – completed his homework. He was in the lead; he was sure of it. Time now to kick for home.

'Now, who wants to go first?' Bob asked.

'Me, I'll go first!' Shey nearly shouted.

'OK, Shey. Please take the hot seat.'

Over the next few minutes, Shey fielded surprisingly friendly questions. Fahad and Kieran asked him about his mimes. Shey was surprised that his competition seemed so docile. Perhaps, they recognized he'd won this and were just being good sports about it? Emi sat silent. Was he plotting something? A payback?

'Shey, I would like to understand why you chose to end *The Story* game the way you did?' asked August.

Ah, here it is, finally, Shey thought. *Fully expected something like this.*

'August, that is quite simple really. I recognized the coded cry for help you and Daisy had written in your first sentences. I thought, how can I help my colleagues? You know we talk a lot about teamwork and collaboration. Of helping one another out. My calculation was simple, the exercise required 250 words and there were no specifics on punctuation. Sometimes I think the role of a team leader is just to fill in any gaps in their team. Like a missing line of code, an unanswered customer call, an incoherent story... the right thing to do is just fill that need. That's what I did.' As Shey finished his final sentence, he stifled a smile. *Wow, this is perfect,* he thought. *I'm on fire today.*

'Shey,' said Emi, unusually softly, 'do you think winning means others must lose?'

'In the immortal words of Ricky Bobby... "If you ain't first, you're last!"' The room groaned. 'You guys don't remember that quote? How about "there may not be a 'U' or 'I' in team... but there is a me!"'... awkward silence... 'Seriously guys. I'm just joking. I think it's important we don't take ourselves too seriously. Of course, we are a team, of course we work toward a common goal. However, sometimes, the role of a leader is to get things done even when it may not be universally popular. Sometimes you are faced with a choice between protecting the status quo, keeping people happy, but at the cost of inaction. I am not afraid to take the bold, unpopular decision even if it ruffles feathers. If I think it's important for the overall success of the business, then I'll do it, even if to some who can't see the bigger picture, I might appear self-centred. The reality is quite the contrary.'

Shey Sinope 4... everyone else 0!

༄༅

Bob looked around at those gathered in the office. It was a little after 6pm. They had wrapped up the day's exercises 30 minutes earlier.

'Well, I think it's a formality don't you all? Mr Canine is expecting our call. Any final thoughts on Shey Sinope?'

'We have the handwriting analysis. Shey's is as we expected,' contributed one colleague.

'Makes sense. Shey came to play today. He clearly had a game plan and executed on that without deviation,' said another of Bob's colleagues.

'Clearly a very high IQ, very driven, very focused,' said another. 'In my view, a classic superhero archetype, very competitive, very clear. But I might venture not his authentic self.'

'Yes, I agree. Incredibly well rehearsed. The Churchillian speech was an interesting flourish. However, we didn't see the real Shey Sinope today. We saw who he thought we wanted to see,' said Julia.

'And the attempts at levity… humour,' said someone else.

'… yes, yes… but… we're all agreed on the recommendation?' said Bob.

He looked around the room and saw several nodding heads.

༄༅

Shey was debating whether to go straight home or head for a self-congratulatory outing. He scanned the downtown neighbourhood. It was still early evening. The sky looked threatening. Perhaps the storm was coming in after all. So much for weather forecasts. He needed to either make straight for home or take shelter somewhere nearby. This part of town typically didn't spring into life until after 10pm. He pictured how it would be later that night. Live music, people spilling out onto the streets. This was the more bohemian part of downtown. Stylish low-rise buildings, a mix of restaurants, bars, comedy, and jazz clubs, and even some notorious drag queen shows.

'Bing.' Shey's phone woke him from his daydream. It was an alert to an incoming email. An urgent message from Ralph Canine. Titled *CAPs Outcome and Next Steps*.

Chey,

I try to reach out to the CAPs participants as quickly as I can after the completion of the assessment. I just finished the de-briefing call with the FAB team.

Lots of good feedback. They see lots of potential. In fact, they think you may be something of a special case. The recommendation though is the CAPs programme is not a good fit for you this year.

I'll send you the more detailed feedback in the next couple of days. We can arrange to meet to discuss any questions you might have.

Have a good evening!

Regards,

Ralph P. Canine Snr (Him/His), EVP HR, SHRM-CP, BSc.

Shey felt numb. A darkness enveloped him. Then he felt it, a slow churning in his stomach. He felt hot, he felt light-headed. The black hole in his stomach just kept getting worse… a knotting of muscles, a bubbling of acid, a witch's cauldron of anxiety, denial, realization, self-doubt. The ravenous monsters of insecurity were fighting to escape their paper-thin prison cell walls. *There you see,* said the monsters, *we always knew you were a failure.*

Shey visualized the indignity of facing people in his office, in his family. The assumptions of success, then, their reactions to learning of his failure. It was too much to bear. He wanted to run and hide.

Shey wasn't sure how long he stood mindlessly on that pavement. Dusk fell, the streetlights blinked into existence. A low growl of thunder rumbled across the sky. Happy for the distraction he thought, *seems Joe Pagan may have got that storm forecast wrong.* The crowd slowly transformed from business suits to more colourful and flamboyant attire. The background noise transitioned from traffic and hushed conversation to music and shouting.

Shey knew he had to move. Movement would help. Perhaps if he could escape this cursed pavement, he could regain his composure. He tested his feet. Slowly, he put one foot in front of the other. A stride, a yard, 100 feet. Once he started, he felt he couldn't stop. He was suddenly aware he didn't know where he was. There was a rowdy crowd straight ahead of him. Suddenly, he was enveloped with drunken revellers.

'What do we have here?' an obviously inebriated, truculent person pointed at him. 'One of those capitalist fat cat bastards who live large while pillaging our natural resources. Wealth is theft… come on everyone…

WEALTH IS THEFT!' His friends joined the chant. It was deafening to Shey. He raised his hands to cover his ears.

'Wait, what is this?… the bastard has one of those stupidly expensive watches on… look!' The obnoxious troublemaker made a grab for Shey's wrist.

What unfolded next happened in blurry slow motion. Shey tried to grab his left hand away but in the process made contact with someone's face. A scuffle ensued. A large clap of thunder rumbled across the sky making everyone flinch. A lightning bolt hit the power transformer on the utility pole above them. A shower of sparking white filament fell around them. Shey felt himself falling to the ground. Before his head hit the pavement, he pressed the red button on his watch.

Beep-beep-beep… beep-beep-beep… was the second last sound Shey remembered. The last was, 'Sashay… is that you… oh dear… Sashay… what kinda lip-sync battle did you get yourself into sweetie?'

Chapter 3

Into the breach once more

'♪♫♫♪♪♫♫♪♫♫'...

Shey opened his eyes, slowly. He was in his bed. He was in his bedroom. He looked around… everything seemed… normal. He turned off the alarm. On his bedside table next to it was… his watch, his completely perfect watch. He ran to his bathroom and checked his reflection.

Well, that's me. Shey checked himself for head trauma. *That's a relief… but also something of a mystery.* He relaxed a little. Whatever had happened the night before, at least it hadn't left him in hospital. He then felt the weight, the sense of loss. *Oh crap… I failed. No escaping that, I suppose.* The feeling in his stomach was still there, in the background, looking for an excuse to rise up and take hold of him.

He tried to distract himself. He made his way back to bed. He picked up his phone and started to surf news, social media, email. Interest rates still up, markets still down, same rumours of some regional banks in trouble… wait, that's crazy, another hurricane? Something seemed off. He slowly built up the courage to look at email. He opened Outlook. Nothing. In fact, no emails from yesterday at all.

'Must have got fried during that fracas last night,' he told himself. He checked his phone's connectivity. An all too familiar occurrence of cloud-based apps and security protocols. While he performed the reboot, deletes, and reloads, log-ons, and authentications, his mind wandered to what must have happened. Perhaps a good Samaritan had intervened and brought him home. He knew this didn't completely make sense. He was wearing his favoured *Robot Wars* t-shirt and Pima cotton *Chirimoya* shorts. The reboot bar completed its last cycle, and he brought his home screen back up.

Wait.... Thursday June 1st? What the hell is wrong with this thing? It's lost a day. Shey reached again for his beloved watch, 'Nooooooo! My watch must have got broken last night. That's heart breaking.'

His phone vibrated.

'Ellen, what day is it? What's the date?'

'Whoa... Shey... are you ok? It's Thursday of course! I was calling to wish you well for your big final day. Break a leg!' Ellen responded.

'Wait. You're sure it's Thursday... not Friday?'

'This is one of your jokes, isn't it?'

'... Yeah... sure....'

So, I guess I just had a very vivid dream? Shey said to himself in the silence that followed his call with Ellen. There was no other explanation. What was it that Sir Arthur Conan-Doyle wrote? 'When you've eliminated the impossible, what remains, however improbable, must be the truth.' It's not like he hadn't had crazy, lifelike dreams before. However, he knew something was off.

I feel like yesterday did happen and that something else is going on.

He got ready for his day rather absent-mindedly. He went through his morning routine and threw on some clothes. If it really was still Thursday, then he was due downtown at the assessment centre.

'Wait… so I haven't failed!' Shey stopped and looked at himself in the mirror. 'OK… come on Shey, pull yourself together!' He scolded his reflection. 'I still have a shot at this…' He broke into a spontaneous rap. He was reminded of the underrated wisdom of *Eminem*.

⁎⁎⁎

With his mind still poring over the events of the morning so far, Shey transported himself from apartment to train. He was so distracted with his thoughts that he almost missed his stop. He made a hasty exit just before the train doors closed.

'I need coffee,' he said.

'One extra-large iced, no whip, non-sugar vanilla, four… wait… make that five-shot, oak milk, café latte, with hemp extract and turmeric, please,' he ordered.

Shey stood to one side and waited for his coffee. Hopefully, this would do the trick.

'Drink for… Sashay… Oooh… nice! Will… SASHAY, please collect their coffee and, by all means Shantay… if you may!' shouted the Barista.

Wait, that can't be a coincidence. All the doubts he had tried to banish from his mind rushed again to the surface. He stood, staring at the Barista.

'I know… it's hard to keep your eyes off me… isn't it? You're not the first to be mesmerized sweetie,' the Barista said. 'Darling, you look like you need a stiff drink… but the best I can offer you is this. You're Sashay, aren't you?'

'Urgh… yarr … me drink… am needy… yes…. not name… but yes…' Shey lost the ability to shape words into regular patterns. 'Look there's an elephant behind you!' Shey tried to distract the Barista, went to snatch the coffee, and make for the door in an ill-conceived attempt to escape any more awkwardness. That's when things took a turn for the worse. As he grabbed the drink… it exploded. He squeezed the cold plastic cup too hard. A fountain of beige shot up to the ceiling and seemed to shower down like lumpy rain. Shey was drenched with iced coffee beverage. A couple of ice cubes rested on one shoulder. Shey froze for a moment. He felt the eyes of the coffee shop on him.

'Oh sweetie. Let me help you.' The Barista rounded the counter towards Shey.

Shey spun on his wet heels. He lunged for the exit, skating on iced beverage shrapnel. He barely kept his feet underneath him. Limbs flying everywhere. The stunned occupants of the coffee shop watched in silent awe as this strange, dishevelled person, wearing his beverage, skidded passed them.

Just before the door closed behind Shey, he heard the Barista say, '… and so just be warned people, that's what happens if you don't tip 20%.'

ᘓᘔ

'Oh dear, Mr Sinope,' said Julia. 'Might I suggest you use the bathroom over there to make yourself feel more comfortable?'

Shey stood in the restroom and took inventory.

OK… deep breaths. Remember, this is a show. Get your head in the game, Shey! He stripped off his shirt and trousers and attempted to rinse the worst of the coffee out in the sink. He spied a powerful hand drier.

'Mr Sinope…?' said Bob, who just emerged from seemingly nowhere.

'Oh… Mr Challack…' Shey tried to think quickly. 'I like to start every day with an iced coffee bath, I find it most invigorating.'

'You don't say,' said Bob as he completed his ritual handwash before quickly exiting.

'I think I rescued that,' Shey said to his reflection.

For the first time today, Shey took a full inventory. He was in one piece despite a disorientating and accident-prone start to the day. While he had not started his day as meticulously as normal, he started to feel more optimistic. *Look, buddy, your hair is a mess, your clothes smell of coffee and oak milk, but you've still got this. Even on a bad day, you can run rings around these people.* He slapped himself a couple of times. *Come on… be the ball Danny… it's hammer time Lewis!*

Shey returned to the reception area and approached Julia. He took his temporary visitor's badge and followed her to the big conference area on the second floor. He took a seat.

'Mr Challack will be with you shortly. We are waiting on the others to arrive before we begin. Feel free to help yourself to coffee… well… presuming you feel up to it.'

'What… again?' Shey asked.

'Yes, well, perhaps that's wise. You may have had enough coffee for one day,' replied Julia. 'I promise it won't be long.'

Shey sat silently as Fahad, August, Kieran, and Daisy arrived. Emi finally breezed in and flamboyantly embraced everyone. Shey's déjà vu radar pinged loudly. Shortly afterward Bob Challack launched into a familiar speech.

'Welcome, everyone!'

As Bob spoke, multiple thoughts fought for primacy in Shey's head. The first was a sense of panic. A sense that things were spiralling. That somehow reality was unfolding. A chasm was appearing in space and time, into which Shey was falling. He couldn't help thinking about Alice in Wonderland as she chased the rabbit into the darkness. Free falling. Then… images of a groundhog invaded his thoughts… and in that other movie… wasn't there an exploding goat? Yes, a goat strapped with dynamite. He shook his head. He frantically checked his surroundings and was only slightly relieved not to spy any out-of-place animals.

Shey hated the feeling of being out of control. He had spent such a long time since college trying to be the master of his own destiny. But that's exactly how this felt. As if the last few years, all that he had built, the immense effort to narrow his world, focus on things he could control, to conquer his career, to prove himself and his worth by 'winning' the corporate game, were becoming a diminishing echo.

Shey suddenly felt on a precipice. Until this moment, he had simply tried to ignore the rather obvious weirdness of this day. He had tried to dismiss the increasing evidence that something strange was happening. Sometimes, when faced with the unexpected you can just keep your head down and buy yourself time. Generally, an explanation presents itself, and in the meantime, you present an outer shell of calm, unflappability, to the world. A widely admired quality in great leaders. Calm rationality in a crisis.

The trouble with this situation was that it just seemed to be getting worse. The more he tried to turn a blind eye, the more the day reached up, grabbed him by the lapels, and slapped him hard across the face.

With the soothing drone of voices as a backdrop, Shey realized that something real was happening or had happened to him. He couldn't dismiss this as pure coincidence. He had heard Bob's speech before. He had spent yesterday with Fahad, August, Kieran, Daisy, and, of course, the annoying Emi. He had met the receptionist *whatshername* yesterday. But it couldn't have been yesterday. Ellen, always the voice of reason, had reassured him that it was simply Thursday... the first time around. So, maybe he'd had one of those 'precognitive' dreams. Where he'd somehow pieced together clues about what was going to happen. All his planning, plotting, research, and rehearsals, had randomly converted into neurons and axons, colliding in some entirely natural way.

Yes, that's it. I've worked so hard to make sure I achieve my goals. I have the formula for success. I've been working incredibly hard, 20 hours a day, seven days a week. It makes sense that all of that will have crept into my subconscious. It's precognition... that's clearly what it is... my mind somehow knew this would happen... snippets of information... data... names... it all gets stored away... an exaflop — a billion-billion mathematical operations per second — the human brain is an amazing thing...

'Because the only other explanation would be that I'm repeating the same day… again… and until I see a goat…'

'… well… that's interesting,' replied Bob. 'And what might be the other two statements you'd like to share with the group. I'm sure you won't be alone in the occasional déjà vu. Or are you meaning in a more existential sense? Like each day of your life feels rather repetitive?'

Everyone was looking at Shey. 'Well, no… what I meant was that… yes, I have lived the same day… twice… yes. When you fly east you see… on Qatar Airlines… flying oryx… which obviously in a certain light can look goatish… entirely possible. Put that down as one of my three.' Shey was scrambling. 'And, yeah, here's a really good one… I invented the word "singularity". That's number two.' That didn't quite sound right. He kept going, sensing that hesitation would make things worse. No… when in doubt, just say something with unequivocal confidence. 'And three… you'll love this… I have a trashcan named Ether.'

The room fell silent. There was a certain awkwardness. Shey's statements had followed the usual anecdotes of brushes with celebrities and stories of extreme sports. However, there had also been tales of childhood traumas, discoveries of long-lost relatives, and a kidney donation.

'My friend Shey... he has lost the plot... no?' The room giggled at Emi's words. 'Maybe, he has invented other words like... how do you say... whack-the-doodle... yes!'

'Or maybe,' said Fahad, 'eccentric...'

'Cray-cray?'

'Interesting... really fascinating. Well, what do you think everyone? Which one is Shey's untruth?' Bob said, sensing a need to move things along. The problem with being a highly skilled industrial psychologist whose day job was babysitting groups of executives participating in the same old exercises was that it got rather monotonous. The answers were always rehearsed, somewhat pat. People always playing games within games. Bob sensed there was something else going on with Shey. *This one may be a bit different after all,* he thought.

Shey retreated into his shell. He started to beat himself up. That was an own goal. And Emi made sure everyone knew about it. *Look, you idiot, you know what's going to happen. You literally know the answers to the final exam! All you have to do is pay attention! And... for God's sake while you're at it... take Emi down!*

Shey Sinope 0... everyone else 1.

∞⊰

'Focus on what's ahead,' Shey told himself. *The 'parts of the elephant' exercise is next. You've got this. Let's just focus on winning!* He started walking toward the door to the Antarctic exhibition simulation. Tacitly urging the room to join him.

'Well… I think we can all agree… a surprisingly interesting little icebreaker…' Bob simultaneously started to lead the group toward the same door.

Boink.

'Oh, so sorry, I beg your pardon,' said Shey as he collided with Bob.

Bob bent down to pick up the papers he had dropped. 'No problem.'

Bob quickly resumed and led them through the door to the snowscape and half-built igloo. He handed out their personal instructions and repeated the simulation objectives and rules. Shey had heard it all before. He rehearsed. *I've lost my voice, but I have instructions to help build the shelter. Fahad and August are snow-blind. Kieran has frostbite in his feet. He can't move. Daisy can't use her hands, and Emi is unconscious! Perfect!*

Shey decided he needed a quick win. He did take a few seconds to survey where the cameras were in relation to his fellow faux Antarctic explorers. He walked over to Kieran. He stood in front of him, and when he was sure he was looking right at him, he pointed at his mouth, scrunched his lips together and made a cross sign. For added emphasis, he opened his mouth and mimed no sound emerging while holding a hand to his ear.

Kieran ignored him.

Shey was stunned. What was he playing at? He persevered. He tried several different attempts to communicate his vocal challenge and the need for him to help corral the others. He contorted his face. He drew messages in the fake snow.

Kieran continued to ignore him.

Shey changed tack. He sprinted over to where Daisy was standing, staring into the distance. He ran through his mimed message.

Daisy ignored him.

Right then Fahad walked up to Shey and mimed his inability to talk. He had an elegance to his hand motions. There was no doubt what he was communicating. Fahad motioned Shey to follow him to where Emi stood next to August who seemed unable to stand. What happened next completely stunned Shey.

'Hey, silly "two truths and a lie" guy, looks like it's just me and August who have some frostbite. Kieran and Daisy are both snow-blind but otherwise able to help us build the shelter. If we can just find the plans… have you seen them?'

It was then that Shey realized he didn't have his personal instructions. He knew Bob had handed them to him. However, well, he hadn't even bothered to look. Shey, took some deep breaths. OK… don't panic. Channel your Sherlock Holmes. Use deduction. Fahad is me, mute. Kieran and Daisy are the old August and Fahad. He stood right in front of a camera and checked off his list.

So snow-blind is taken. Mime is taken. Frostbite… that is August and Emi. So that leaves… The penny dropped. He gazed toward the ceiling… Crap… Crap… Crap… Crap… Crap… Crap… Crap…

Shey Sinope 0… everyone else 2.

࿇ఎఢ

Bob got the group ready for *The Story* exercise. He explained… again… the ground rules. Short story, written by committee. Shey sat morosely. *This is a disaster,* he thought. *Is there even any point now?* He heard a little voice shout back: *Yes! remember this has been a three-day process. You aced everything up until now. Just finish strong. Remember MGL Mania love you! Ultimately, this is supposed to be a coronation.*

'I'm beginning to lose hope,' Shey muttered. 'I don't know I have anything left. I feel… drained.'

'… and I think… yes… Shey, why don't you pair with… umm… Daisy and … Emi.'

Bob invited them to begin, he walked over to their table. 'Shey, why don't you go first?'

Shey looked at the blank paper, it looked back at him accusatorially. He looked at Fahad, then Emi. Shey wanted to blame Emi. Lay all the twists, faux pas, and his corresponding downward spiral at his feet. He reached for the pencil.

'I'm taking you guys down with me, PYJAMA faces!' he wrote. How did that make sense? Including the senseless word in a sentence clearly designed to derail them all. *This is all too surreal. As much as Emi took advantage of the situation, I blew myself up today.*

He erased the sentence. Then wrote:

'If today is yesterday, does that mean tomorrow will be today? Or will it still be yesterday… again? Here is what I do know. Today has not gone very well for me. I thought today was going to be one of the most important in my life. I think I was right, but not for the reasons I thought.

Something else is happening to me… and apparently just me. I'm in a sort of purgatory, a limbo, or precognitive prison. However, before I go, let me make sure you know that Emi is not a nice person and I hope he doesn't win. Now, I think I'd like to go home now. Yes, I think that's what I'm going to do.'

Shey stood up, walked to the door, and exited.

༄༅

Shey didn't remember exactly how he left the assessment centre. He had reached a tipping point. It was all too much. He walked the early evening city streets. It was familiar and strangely comforting. The buzz of traffic. The animated chatter of businesspeople rushing to catch their trains. He marvelled at the poetic beauty. There was a gentle choreography to how people moved. A soundtrack with a distinct beat. It soothed him.

He had failed today, bombed, flopped, crashed, and burned. Everything he touched, everything he tried, blew up in his face. The whole Thursday do over… well, as much as he had tried to use it as an advantage… it just ended up being the reverse. He also had this feeling of everything appearing ethereal, dreamlike, unreal. Like the day was a giant movie set, or simulation. He thought of *The Truman Show*.

Shey couldn't shift his thinking from the assessment day. He knew, deeply, that something more important, more seismic was happening. He had a sense that a colossal, cosmic force was exerting itself on him. But it was just easier to ignore it and focus on how he had screwed up his big shot… again. *What pisses me off the most about today was that I knew what was going to happen and still screwed it up. I had the biggest advantage possible… but fumbled the ball. I should have killed today… instead I ended up conspiring to find amazingly inventive ways to shoot myself in both feet. And Emi… jeez… he will have loved how it went.*

His phone pinged. Shey didn't bother to read it. He knew what it said.

Shey felt drained, exhausted. The uncertainty and anxiety he felt when he was at university had been frightening. At the time he needed to fill it with something that gave him a sense of worthiness, of identity. His career at MGL Mania had been the answer. He realized his failure was amplified by what his career meant to him. Shey was his job. The identities were inseparable. There wasn't anything else.

Once again, he started to wallow and think about how his 'failure' would be judged. How his status and value would be reduced. He raised his head to the darkening skies. *I've failed… again… but even I would have failed me today. What is wrong with me?* A familiar voice replied… *Shey, you know you've always been a loser. The fact is you never deserved any of this anyway. You just stretched the law about fooling some of the people all of the time but not all of them all of the time. This day was long overdue. It's time to accept that you don't deserve success.*

The comfortable, warm embrace of despondency washed over him. He watched the skies turn darker and angrier, matching his mood. Like a giant visualizer paired to his brain patterns. He heard a rumble of thunder overhead. He opened his arms, closed his eyes.

'I had my shot… but it just went south… I can't control my mouth… just no clout… three strikes… and out… OUCH!'

'I hate amateur street corner rappers,' said the man at the end of the fist. 'It's cultural appropriation… lacks authenticity. I bet you're a Vanilla Ice fan as well… right… we'll give you a reason to shout about icicles!' The hip-hop snob turned to his crowd of friends and gestured to help him teach Shey a painful lesson. They engulfed Shey and jostled him back and forth. Shey fell to the ground. He instinctively grabbed for his watch. He pressed the red button.

Beep-beep-beep… beep-beep-beep…

'Sashay… is that you?' It was the Barista, looking flamboyantly different. With superhuman power they cut a path through the rowdy self-appointed, hip-hop police, grabbed Shey and carried him to safety.

'I'll be killing your little brains like a poisonous viper… sniper… an avenging pied piper,' the Barista stunned the rowdy crowd. 'Now remember… or I'll toast you all… roast you… and I don't boast… word!' To Shey, 'Don't worry honey. These guys don't stand a chance in any back-and-forth rap battle.' Those were the last words Shey remembered. Ions built around him. The hairs on his body stood up. A bolt of pure energy struck a power transformer somewhere close. Hot filament showered down around them. Darkness followed.

Chapter 4

Whether to suffer the breaches of outrageous fortune

'♩♫♫♩♫♩♫♫♩♫♫'...

Shey opened one eye then the other. He spied, gingerly, his surroundings. Once again, he had been transported to his bedroom. The strange discontinuity and unexplained teleportation from melee, electrical storm, and drag queen rescue, to his bedroom lingered in his mind. However, priorities, he turned to look at his phone. Then he searched for his watch.

Thursday... again... again. No doubt. No doubt at all. Shey just kept repeating the same words. He felt the walls closing in. A tsunami of panic rushed towards him. He pulled the bed sheets up over his head and started to scream. Shey felt simultaneously under attack from some mysterious malevolent force and incredibly lonely. *What's happening to me, who is doing this to me, why am I being tortured like this, what have I done to deserve this... this...* His thought was interrupted by a phone call.

'Hey Shey, I was calling to wish you well for your big final day. Break a leg!' Ellen's cheerful, sane, calm, normal voice, was like an island to a shipwreck survivor. Shey grasped for it.

'Ellen, I think I'm living the same day over and over again,' Shey confided.

'Well, I think we all feel like that sometimes, Shey,' Ellen responded.

'I don't mean like humdrum, boring, repetitive in that sense. No, I mean for real. I have lived this day, Thursday June 1st, at least twice already. This is the third time around. It's like I'm caught in a time warp, some sort of *Groundhog Day*.' Shey found speaking with Ellen helped calm him.

'Like you're Bill Murray? And you're forced to work through something important before you can move on?' Ellen detected Shey needed her to play along. 'Honestly, Shey, it's more likely you have some post-REM sleep delusion. I read recently about sleep paralysis. It's a real thing. You're probably experiencing a vivid echo from a dream where you re-lived the day.'

'I know how this sounds, but I'm definitely in a time loop. Do you think it's likely to be Bill Murray-esque, or more *Quantum Leap?* They were different constructs. There was also that recent *Palm Springs* movie where they had to blow up a goat in a cave to escape the time bubble.'

'I suspect you are building up to a punchline. I'm being drawn into a classic Shey Sinope joke here.'

'Basically, if you boil them down though, they all had one thing in common. The protagonists had to find something. Something elusive. Something important. Something needing to be put right. Yes… makes sense!' Shey's power to reason, to try to make sense of his situation, gave him hope. Helped him swim to the surface. 'It must be the assessment… that must be the key… if I get them to pass me… then I get to move on… has to be!'

'OK you've lost me. If that was one of your jokes… I didn't get it. But, as far as the assessment goes… good luck!'

‰Ↄჾ

Days 4–30: Rinse and repeat

Shey, with renewed enthusiasm and commitment, threw himself back into the assessment centre. He had to pass the test to move on with his life. He needed to get his deserved career accolade. He thought about the variables and decided to systematically work through them.

At first, he dove straight back in where he left off. He knew the games. He knew the rules. He knew the players. He even had a suspicion that he may have intrigued Bob in some way. However, it just didn't work. He got close a couple of times to what he considered perfect execution of the games, a perfect performance, showcasing just how good he was. He even managed to neutralize Emi. And yet, each evening he got the same 'Dear Chey' failure email.

He concluded that his approach must be wrong. He tried to revalidate his foundational success formula. He thought if he exaggerated different parts that might help. One day he just focused on visible effort, and the next smart insights. To his surprise, and disappointment, the closest he came to success was when he exaggerated compliance… just playing each game strictly based on the instructions. In all cases, though, the same message from Ralph Canine.

Finally, he threw the formula out. It just didn't work for the assessment day. However good it had been in the office, there was a different dynamic in this simulated environment. He spent some days trying to figure out what other tactics might work. He tried a mirroring approach, where he copied what others did and said. Fail. He tried to manipulate who he worked with and the different roles he could get in the games. Fail. He even invested a few days to watch what the others did and select the best for him to copy the next day. Fail.

As the days went by, Shey's enthusiasm started to evaporate. Something wasn't right. He did as much analysis and review as he could. There were some constraints and limitations. For example, whatever he did, his days always started at 6am. When he woke, the only evidence of the previous day was in his head. Everything else got reset. At the other end of each day, around 9pm, no matter what he tried, he always ended up being confronted by a truculent crowd, a violent electrical storm, and a really well-dressed good Samaritan. He thought the evening curfew should have been easy to fool. He was wrong. He had been beaten up in the middle of an apparently deserted park, where revellers mysteriously appeared and engulfed him. On another occasion he tried to escape the city by train only to be accosted between train stations. Shey recalled some of the strangely inventive taunts and provocations he had heard:

'I hate rhetorical word devices. Why ask the question if you already know the answer? Damn Greeks… apart from

Pericles of course... now he was an oratory genius... YOU, however... you're just bloody irritating...!'

He had been struck by lightning inside buildings, on the subway, one very embarrassing occasion in a bathroom, and even inside a shopping mall while attempting to purchase thick rubber-soled Dr Martins. He remembered the surreal image.

'Sashay... oh no darling... those are not the footwear you are looking for!' said the Barista looking splendid in their evening attire, as a salesperson approached with a box of 1460 boots in a size 11. The store lights flickered, there was a boom, and somehow a bolt of lightning appeared through the store window.

The other thing consistent with every evening, was the reassuring sound of his international SOS signal. Shey clung to the belief that his watch helped protect him in some fashion. He lost consciousness each evening to the *beep-beep-beep... beep-beep-beep...*

ഓഃ

Day 31: Plumbing the depths

'There can only be one logical conclusion. Bob and his team are out to get me. I am in some kind of purgatory. Penalized for being clearly the most talented, well-prepared, smartest person in the room. Whatever I do, they will fail me out of sheer jealousy. Yes, that's the only thing that makes sense. I've killed those assessments... several times now.' Shey was talking to the reflection in his bathroom mirror. He looked terrible. Manic. 'But how deep does the conspiracy go? Is it just FAB or has Canine told them to fail me? I must find out... I must break the cycle. There is no other way out!'

He confronted Bob in the assessment centre offices. Armed with a sex-triplet iced coffee and dressed in his pyjamas, Shey stormed past Julia and confronted Bob in his office.

'You're going to tell me the answers to the tests, Bob. One way or the other. You're going to tell me and then, tomorrow, I'm going to come down here and win!' Shey stood in Bob's office doorway.

'Shey, you do not look well. Did something happen to you last night? Should I call for medical assistance?' Bob pressed a button under his desk. He had it installed a couple of years back after an unfortunate incident following some ill-advised consulting engagements.

'Look, an elephant!' Shey pointed.

Successfully distracted, Shey managed to bundle Bob out of his office. He then barricaded the door. He searched through Bob's desk and filing cabinets, before realizing Bob had left his laptop unlocked. Shey searched the files and found notes on him and the other participants.

෪෯

'You have the right to remain silent. Anything you say may be used in evidence against you…' A disconcertingly tall police person was reading Shey his rights. The FAB office occupants gawped as Shey was led through the offices to the awaiting squad car.

Shey couldn't get the words he'd read out of his head. 'Shey Sinope is undoubtedly smart, undoubtedly driven. In the tests this week, Shey has scored in the upper quartile across the slate. In many respects, he represents the strong, single-minded, narcissistic leader that many companies select for executive leaders. The key question is whether Shey's emotional immaturity will be too great a burden for him if he goes any further without a course correction. We intend to look at this closely on the last day. However, in our view, it is highly likely he will confirm rather than confound our analysis.

'Unless Shey confronts the questions he's hiding from, we believe he may be on a course toward self-destruction. But it is avoidable. His bigger questions are those of who he really is, what fulfils him, what he really wants to do with his life, and how he can build a healthier, deeper self-image. It is evident that he currently engages at a very transactional and superficial level. He draws a sense of worth from workplace competition. He treats it all like a game. A game, we might add, that he is very good at. It may be that MGL Mania still choose to include Shey in the CAPs programme, but we think that for Shey's longer-term benefit, it would be far better to force him to confront these questions now, while he has the time to make healthier choices.'

৪০৫৪

Day 32–50: Capitulation

'♫♫♫♫♫♫♫♫♫♫'...

Shey reached over, picked up his phone, and threw it out of the window. The window wasn't open. It made a huge crash and fell to the ground. Five minutes later, it began to ring again. He got up, walked into his living room, opened a drawer, picked something up, walked back into his bedroom, and then murdered his phone with a hammer.

What was the point? Bob and FAB had seen through him. How did they manage it? It didn't matter. Reading Bob's notes was like reading an open letter into his soul. *If my Bill Murray challenge is to defeat the assessment, I'm doomed,* he thought. *There's no escaping my destiny.*

Shey spent the next few days morosely in his own company. Ellen called every morning, and he declined the call. Julia from FAB started to call from about 9.30am. She called three times by 11am and then stopped. Around midday people from MGL Mania started to call. He ignored them all. Around 9pm he heard voices outside his apartment door.

'I hate hermits, but what I hate more are morose, self-indulgent, self-loathing hermits.' This was followed by a group of five or six people entering his apartment and a spectacular electric storm that looked beautifully deadly from his apartment window.

Beep-beep-beep... beep-beep-beep...

'Sashay... there you are... where have you been all day long? Don't worry sugar, I'll get rid of these idiots for you... everything will be ok... Barbie's here. Clear off you lot or you'll make Barbie mad... and trust me... rainbow glitter anger doesn't easily wash off!'

୫୦୯୪

Day 50–100: Taking a break

'♪♫♫♪♪♫♫♪♫♫'...

I need a vacation. It was 6am on Thursday, June 1st. *I have 15 hours. Ummmm...*

Over the next few weeks, Shey got into a routine of booking a plane ticket on his phone and heading for a different destination. He always flew first class, had limo transfers, and stayed in the best hotels. If you put aside the whole world resetting, annoyingly persistent rowdy crowd and violent electrical storm that seemed to follow him, it wasn't a bad deal. He always woke up the next day right back where he started with the memory but none of the expense. Through trial and error, he found destinations he could reach in under four hours, giving him enough time to see a little of a new place.

He had some incredibly exotic meals, stayed at some very exclusive resorts, bumped into some reasonably famous celebrities, and drank some strange and wonderful cocktails. After a few days, he started to look forward to two parts of his day. To his surprise, it wasn't the small sense of being able to escape his looped 24 hours by flying to surprise destinations. Nor was it the pampering he received from the people who thought they were charging him $15,000 a night. In fact, the faux hospitality started to grate quite quickly.

What he really looked forward to each day was speaking with Ellen each morning. Even though she would have no memory of the calls, he had become deeply interested in what she was doing, how her work at the NGO was going. It was like a Netflix mini-series that he'd just discovered. He was on Season 1, and he hoped there were at least three or four more.

The second was at 9pm. There was a back story to Barb the Barista. He wanted to understand what it was.

‹‹‹ ☙ ›››

Day 100 onwards: A search for connection – time with Ellen

'Hey Shey, I was calling to wish you well for your big final day. Break a leg!'

'Thanks Ellen. Say, what are you up to today?' Shey replied.

'Well, I'm trying to help my NGO think up new ways to soften the negative impacts of social media, particularly on teens and pre-teens. I've a pitch deck I'm working on today. Plan to review it with the founder next week. I'll probably bury myself in it today. Work from home. So, you'll call me this evening with a de-brief? I want to hear how it went.'

Shey had heard most of this before during their daily calls.

'So, if I were sitting in the coffee shop across the street from your apartment ordering drinks, would you want one?'

Ten minutes later they sat at a table with their drinks.

'What brings this on?' Ellen asked.

'Are you willing to be completely open minded? Let me tell you something incredibly fantastic? The thing is I know I have given you cause over the years to think when I start to say something, launch into a monologue, I am building up to a joke, or a diatribe on a pet subject. I need you to believe me right now when I say I am going to be honest, vulnerable, and sincere.' Shey held Ellen's gaze.

'Shey, despite what you may think, I do always listen to you. I have this strange belief that at some stage you are going to make some breakthrough and the real Shey Sinope will emerge. So, go ahead.'

'Over the past few months, something extraordinary has been happening to me. It's crucial for me to be able to share this with you and to prove to you that it's true. In this moment, there is only one thing that matters to me, and that's whether the strength of our friendship can bridge a fantastic leap of faith. The thing is, I honestly don't think I've done anything to deserve that kind of faith. But… well… you are sort of my best friend.' Shey's voice wobbled.

Shey explained the daily reset, the daily routine, how it began, how it continued. He explained what happened at the assessment centre. What happened at the end of each day.

'I've been to the library, searched the top theoretical physicists' research, corresponded with top scientists, discussed it with local and regional clergy, watched all the movies, and, honestly, beyond describing the phenomenon, there is no explanation. But it's true. And I can prove it to you.' Shey paused to see if Ellen was still with him. Her face suggested she remained intent, vested, waiting for the punchline. 'Over the past couple of months, we have spoken every day. For you it was the same day. However, for me, well, I asked you what would convince you that someone was living the same day over and over again. You said it would be easy to prove, they'd just need to know the answer to these five questions about you, your life, and your family. Things that could never be found out on the internet or by your run-of-the-mill stalker. Well… here are the answers. You gave me these over the last few weeks.'

Ellen looked at Shey's handwritten list. She scanned the questions.

'OK Shey… as crazy as this sounds… I'll do this. I believe you. Call it an experiment or probation. If this is true… there are probably some other things you can do to prove it.'

'Yes, well, I knew you'd say that. And in anticipation of your next thought and suggestion, here is a list of all the major things that will happen today, from 8am through 9pm. I've broken the list down into major news events, sports scores, weather, even what the next five people in the coffee shop will say to one another... starting in... three... two... one.'

Ellen watched in awe as Shey predicted exactly what the next five people ordered. How the staff responded. Even how one lady got the wrong order and kicked up a fuss. Then, right on cue, a man fell off his bicycle right outside. All on Shey's notes.

'How many times have we had this conversation?' Ellen asked.

Shey smiled.

Shey felt something shift. Ellen, as always, believed in him. Even the most fantastic, outlandish, unbelievable, and she was still willing to give him the benefit of the doubt. When a friend is asked to choose between rationality and you, and they pick you... well, that's a special kind of bond.

Each day, going forward, Shey met an unsuspecting Ellen for coffee. Each day she renewed her alliance, shared his repetitive calendar, and spent time brainstorming what he should do. They agreed there must be a hidden key, a hidden quest, which might be the answer to releasing Shey. Shey's mission was to find it and conquer it. They agreed he needed to look in some new places and ask some new questions. The assessment day, joining CAPs, they thought might be a red herring. It was too obvious. And, of course, Shey had tried that and failed... repeatedly.

ೞ◌ೞ

Day 101 onwards: A search for connection – the Barista's story

Shey sat in his favourite post-Ellen meeting spot. He enjoyed watching the hustle and bustle of the world. From his seat by the window, he saw people hurry into his second coffee shop of the day. They placed their orders and waited impatiently. Shey estimated at least half of the patrons never looked up from their phones. It was as if each inhabited a bubble of their own insular reality. A smartphone bubble... a *phubble*. Occasionally, someone would be confronted with the unwelcome necessity to physically interact outside their phubble. They would scowl and look irritated.

'They're like little robots, aren't they?' said the Barista.

'Yes, I think that was me a few months ago,' replied Shey. 'It's interesting isn't it? Like each day we go to work, we go locked in our phubbles. Protecting ourselves by shielding ourselves from the insidious evil of the corporate treadmills. Sedating ourselves with dopamine hits from social media likes and 30-second videos.'

'Quite the urban philosopher! I think "social" media has had quite the opposite impact. Rather than make us more social, it has amplified our isolation. The even sadder thing is that it's eroded our ability to feel empathy for others. The insidious erosion of our ability to relate, to be kind. Oh, for the good old days when people socialized in groups, physically, and shared experiences in reality, rather than via headsets!'

'Now who's the social philosopher!' Shey laughed. And then added idly, 'Maybe we should try to fix that.

Seems like a noble pursuit. Must be a solution.' He looked a little into the distance. 'Can I ask you a question?'

'Shoot Sashay cutey, how can I say no to that sweet innocent cherub face?'

'How did you decide what career or profession you'd follow? Did you have a clear sense of what you wanted to do? And does it make you happy?'

'Well, that's more than one question. My feeling is that the question may be back to front. Rather than ask about profession or career, there are other more important questions that you have to work through first. In my case, I dreamed of performing, being an entertainer. Like many people in my industry, you then have to decide how much you're prepared to sacrifice for that dream. I need to pay rent, pay some bills. That's why I work here. I just don't make enough money from my Babs the Barista alter ego to make ends meet. But I tell you Sashay, when I'm on stage... when the audience and I are communing... it's something sacred... something spiritual. I truly think I was put on this earth to entertain, and to make people laugh. And I love every minute of it.' Babs' eyes sparkled.

Shey spent most of his mid-mornings in Babs' company. They were wise, witty, insightful, and above all, very kind. Shey marvelled how this happened without any need to explain being trapped in a time loop. It was natural. They talked about everything from work, to family, friends, and dreams. Shey confided he never understood when people talked of following their dreams. The only equivalent he could muster were just unattainable fantasies. Just flights of fancy, things he could only ever construe as pure escapism.

'The trouble with that approach to life is that you deny yourself the possibility. A famous philosopher once said life is about hope, the dream of a better tomorrow. The chance to do something you really want to do; not what others make you do. Something that's yours and yours alone.' One of the things Shey liked about Babs was their willingness to listen and discuss anything. They never made Shey feel like there was any judgement. 'Look at me. If I hadn't followed my dreams, I would have been trapped by that offer to join the Wall Street Bank graduate programme. Can you imagine? Me... in a suit... looking at high frequency trading algorithms. I dodged a bullet there... for sure!'

Shey thought back to his nerdy days playing with toy robots and software programming. He loved constructing models and testing them in the arena. What was it about that that he loved? He knew why he stopped. It just wasn't... cool. In his teens, it was sort of like chess club... you made a choice between taking a merciless ribbing from all the popular kids in school or you cut your losses and tried to appear less of a target.

ಬಂಡ

Day 102 and occasionally onwards: A search for meaning – time with Uncle Freddy

Shey started to call Uncle Freddy around lunchtime. Shey found he was available to talk between various pet projects. He hated to be labelled 'retired'. He insisted he was just going through another phase of reinvention.

'How's my favourite nephew today? You must be desperate to call me in the middle of your day. No underlings to torture?' What a wit.

'Now, as your only nephew, that isn't a huge accolade. Just for a second, would you humour me? If you think back to my formative years, what do you think I was good at? What sorts of things did you think made me happy?'

'Well, that's an easy question. You loved making things. I often thought you'd be some sort of engineer. But perhaps those labels aren't what you're looking for. No, if I think about when you were at your happiest, it's when you had made something or when you had solved a problem you saw around the house. Your Mum and Dad would often show me some of the sketches and ideas you used to draw for them. Everything from self-making beds to the legendary robot trashcans. Yes, I'd say the essence of that was you trying to automate chores your parents insisted you do. Sadly, all those harebrained ideas evaporated a bit during high school and college.'

It was true... to a degree. Even in college he continued to play with kit building and little inventions. But he hid them away. It was very apparent that everyone around him was working hard to get coveted internships in graduate programmes with banks, technology, marketing, or energy companies. The career treadmill seemed like an arms race. It also felt like everyone else's definition of success.

Over the coming days, in his conversations with Uncle Freddy he explored different exercises he might practise to help him reconnect with his happier, former past. To see if it let him rekindle the joy, the freedom, he used to feel. A benefit of being stuck reliving the same day is that nothing you do is permanent. The mistakes are easily remedied. Shey resolved to find something he enjoyed, that he had a conviction about. Something he was prepared to fight for. He wanted to see if he could find his version of Babs' story.

ಬಂಡ

Day 102 and sporadically afterward: A search for meaning – time with Mum and Dad

Shey found time to connect with his parents in the early evening. He had never been enthusiastic about deep conversations with them. Do you ever stop worrying about what your parents think of you? It makes it super complicated to broach an honest discussion about who you are and what you might want to do.

But this strange *groundhog effect* was liberating.

'Mum, is Dad around?' Shey knew he would be. They were very much the double act.

'Yes, he's right here.' With the mouthpiece muffled, 'It's Shey calling. He sounds like he's in a coffee shop.'

'Mum, I have a question for you. Was it you and Dad's dream for me to go be a senior executive for some big business? Is that what you both wanted for me?'

'No… I think something is up with Shey.' Mum did a poor job of muffling the phone before shoving Dad on.

'Everything alright son? Don't mind your Mum. She's ever the protective mother. I heard your question. I'd say yes but also no. Yes, of course, we are delighted you've done so well with your career these past few years. Every parent wants their kid to make that tough transition to standing on their own two feet. And every parent believes their child is special and capable of reaching higher, higher than their parents, and yes, higher than other kids. I think that may be a cave-age or Darwinian inbuilt thing.'

Mum grabbed the phone back and completed his thought for him.

'What Dad means is, we just want you to be happy, but in the process, we can't help but hope that you don't make any big mistakes. We both are impressed by what you've done at MGL Mania… but there is no doubt in our minds you could have done that anywhere… perhaps a place that allows you more time for a personal life. What matters most is that you prove that to yourself.'

'Mum, are you angling for me to spend less time at work and more time finding someone who can help you become a grandma?'

'I didn't say that. No, but you have been so consumed by work. Maybe you should spend more time thinking about what else you want from life. A family is a part of that. But all work, work, work, ultimately must be unfulfilling. When will you have time to enjoy any of the rewards?'

೮೦೦೪

Day 151: A new hope

Shey checked his watch. It was 8:59pm.

'Welcome… come in… help yourself.' Shey pointed the small crowd to the beautiful buffet. 'And over in the corner of the living room, Lars here will get you some drinks. He makes a great Mocktini!'

'Well… this doesn't seem right. Every instinct in my body still says I should dislike you.'

'Now, now. Why must there be hostilities? Look outside, a terrible storm rages. In here it's warm, dry, there are refreshments, and… drum roll… entertainment… let me introduce, fresh from their residency at Divines Downtown Dive… where they got rave reviews… the one and only… the gorgeous, glorious, incomparable, Babs the Barista!' A DJ fired up the music, balloons cascaded from the ceiling, and a spotlight found Babs' statuesque form, smiling broadly.

'Good evening my lovelies… have I got a night of surprises in store for you…'

CRACK… BOOM… CRACK CRACK… BOOM BOOM…

Beep-beep-beep… beep-beep-beep…

Chapter 5

A breach is what you make it

'♪♬♬♪♪♬♬♪♬♬'…

She swung out of bed. He had taken to starting each day to a new soundtrack. He switched the music on and sang along. He needed something that amplified his sense of being lost but now found. Of being disorientated by an impenetrable fog, but now starting to make out familiar landmarks through the haze. Miss Swift was a genius in conjuring such a feeling. She captured his emotions perfectly.

He had work to do. Conversations, debates, passionate arguments. Questions, he had many questions. And an idea… one big idea. There was excitement, possibilities, a cause, a compelling enquiry. Of course, it was still Thursday, still June 1st, but he no longer worried about that. He didn't check his phone or watch. They had become less important.

He bounded into his bathroom and got ready for his day.

☙❧

Day 152 onwards: Opening new avenues of enquiry

'Uncle, are you out on your morning walk?' Shey knew Uncle Freddy was an early riser.

'Yes, Shey. Chuckles is getting on a bit, just like me, but he does enjoy our morning constitutional. The world always seems at its most cheerful and peaceful in the morning. The possibilities still lie ahead, perfect, yet to be spoiled by humanity's well-meaning but typically ham-fisted bungling.'

'Do you think there's an empathy deficiency in the world?'

'Of course. That's like asking are we experiencing global warming. Only the absolutely committed, die-hard, bone-headed, flat-earth conspirators, would even debate it.'

'What if we could change that? What if I had an idea to use our addiction to social media, to the virtual world, as a means to turn the tide on empathy? Would that be a good thing? It would, wouldn't it?'

'A big yes with a small qualification. Just remember a deficiency is bad but so too can be an abundance. It's about balance. Tell me, though, is this about addressing the world's empathy deficiency, or your own?' Uncle Freddy did not suffer from an empathy deficiency.

'I do feel uncomfortable dealing with my own emotions, let alone others'. It's just easier to bottle them up and ignore them.'

'Ah Shey. But what happens when bottles have combustible things stored in them, particularly if they get shaken?'

৪০০৪

Day 175 onwards: Something intriguing this way comes

'Let me get this straight,' Ellen said, scratching her head and pointing at the pencil drawing on the napkin. 'It's a virtual reality headset?'

'Well, no… but also… yes. It's not so much how people will label it that's all that important. It's more what it does. I've been spending the last few weeks looking to try to make social media… well, more social. It struck me that the problem is that there's no emotional connection. So, I've fixed that. I've found a way to create real emotional connections. The design means that anyone wearing it will experience the emotional responses to their actions. Direct and instant feedback on the *consequences* of their words and deeds. The bigger the impact, the stronger the experience. It's a *Feedback Emotional Enhancement Loop*.' Shey pointed to the diagram where he had scribbled some software shorthand and copper connections designed to rest on frontal lobes. 'I'm calling it the *FEEL VR* set.'

'Well, I love the idea. I see the potential. It could radically change people's behaviour. But why would people choose to wear it? Sadly, I think people like to throw anonymous rocks via the internet.'

'Well, I think I've got some ideas about that. First, I think as a product it has to be innocuous, not like one of those crazy ski-goggle sized monstrosities. That's why I think it should just be the size of a travel sickness sticker… just have to put one either side of your temple…

here and here,' he cut two pieces of the napkin out and held them up to Ellen. 'Your hair would obscure them most of the time.

'Second, the beauty of the idea is that it stimulates all your emotions. It's still an idea at this stage. I need to build the prototype and test it. But while I'm coming into this thinking about empathy... let's just say... I believe it would enhance ALL the normal human emotions.' He looked at Ellen and saw the penny drop.

'Wow... really. That would be... very, very, very popular!' Ellen's face was a dramatic animation as she worked through all the implications. 'OH... MY... GOD... people would LOVE these things. You couldn't make enough of them!'

'I know! The other thing is, it's my belief I can produce these cheaply. The hardware that is. A lot of this is the software AI programming. But... and this is where I really think it's elegant... once I've programmed it... it's done. It just learns and grows and improves itself. I'll need to host the neural network... and people will need to use their existing broadband... but that's about it. Just imagine, if I can find a way to manufacture the patches for less than $10... and the software is just my time... well, what would you prefer... a $3,000 pair of goggles that replicate what your phone does... or unreal *amplified* emotional stimulation for next to nothing?'

⊱⊰

Day 175–200: If all you have is a hammer, everything looks like a nail

'No… not that way. That's not what I told you to do. Are you stupid? Give it to me.' *Clearly, they just let anyone wander in off the street and join these invention workshops,* Shey thought.

'Shey, can I have a word?' Tony was the leader-cum-organizer of the workshop. Shey had found the inventors' workshop online and spent most of his afternoons using their equipment. He'd made little progress developing his prototype. He had faced two major challenges: the first was finding the components he needed and the second was finding some good lab assistant's help.

'Yes… sure. Can you make it snappy though? I've got things to do and only so many hours before CRACK… BOOM… *Beep… Beep… Beep…* time.'

'I'm afraid we have to ask you to leave. There have been too many complaints. It's amazing that in the three hours since I first met you, you have been able to alienate everyone in the workshop. You do understand this is a cooperative… a volunteer organization? We get the best talent from the local technical university in here, but I'm sincerely worried that if we allow you to stay, we won't be so much a collaborative as a sole proprietorship. And not a benevolent one at that.'

Shey was consumed by the idea. He had an intoxicating feeling about it. A feeling of something important, world changing. It should be obvious that everything, anything else paled by comparison. He shouldn't need to explain or cajole. But every day he ended up with people getting angry and denying him the resources he needed. It didn't help that he had to construct his model from scratch each day. He had 15 hours in which to build something. That was not a lot of time.

He left the workshop and went over to Babs' coffee shop. It was late afternoon, but he hoped he wouldn't miss the end of their shift. He arrived just as they were leaving.

'Babs, can you spare a few minutes to give me some advice?'

'For you Sashay, of course. I'm not due on stage until 9.30pm tonight.'

'I have this great idea, great design, for a new product. I think it's really important, really necessary. But I'm struggling to get people to help me build it. I need to find a way to get people to do what I want. I need them to just do what I tell them. Isn't that how all the big innovations were famously born, by the strength of a founder's personality? Bend reality around them or something. So, how do I do that?'

'Not sure that's my domain, Sashay. I can tell you that one certain way NOT to get people to help you is to try to FORCE them to do so. That's basic human psychology. I suspect you aren't going about this the right way. Have you tried different approaches?'

'When I think about the big leaders back at MGL Mania, when they wanted something done, well they just told people to do it and they did it. People complied. That hasn't worked for me. Then, there's the whole carrot and stick approach. I have promised people financial reward, but they have typically thought I was either joking or some sort of con artist. It's just hard for people I've just met to feel confident my offers are genuine... which I guess... maybe they aren't. And I've also tried the stick approach of various levels of threat. Not proud of myself but, you know, the ends justify the means.'

'OK... let me stop you there. This is above my pay grade Sashay. But what I will say is you can't treat people on a purely transactional basis. You are framing this wrong. You should ask yourself why someone would want to help you. If you get a good answer to that, then you're a long way toward solving your problem.'

&∞03

Day 175 onwards: Contemplating Pandora's box

Shey began to take some bigger risks. He found those old, unwritten social boundaries became less and less important. He had always abided by the unspoken rule that we don't share our true feelings, doubts, and anxieties. It was liberating to let them out. He increasingly opened up to Uncle Freddy, Ellen, Babs, and anyone who would listen, with questions, doubts, and even feelings.

'I've always feared looking more deeply at who I am. It's hard to believe that anyone, including me, could really love or even like that person. Over the years, I've found it's easier to leave whoever they are locked away. It's surprisingly easy to do that. Just banish them. Work can be a powerful cloak of invisibility. People conflate who you are with your job.'

'Can you pass the salt, please?' said the distinguished looking gentleman next to Shey. He had reminded him of a ghost he had once dreamed about, a long time ago.

'You look like someone who knows who they are. What's your secret? Your story? Did you ever run away from a fear of finding out something about yourself?'

The person sitting the other side of Shey said, unexpectedly, 'Yes. Yes, I have. You aren't alone, young man.' She was an elderly woman, perhaps in her 70s. 'The trouble though is that if you never try to understand yourself, never pluck up the courage to find out what you like, who you love, and what makes you happy… well… by definition… you will never be happy. Ask yourself this, would you rather know and accept even the worst possible discovery about yourself, if in turn it gave you the opportunity, but not the guarantee, of unconstrained bliss?'

৪৩

Day 200 onwards: Adding a new dimension to Bob Challack (and Julia) – part 1

'We're not expecting you until 9am, Mr Sinope.' Julia was surprised to find Shey waiting for her.

'I know. It's just I was hoping to get a few minutes with Bob before the day began. I have some questions about work. I thought if anyone might have some good advice it would be you guys.'

'Bob will be in around 7.30am. Why don't you come in. I'm happy to listen in the meantime. If I better understand what you're struggling with I might be able to point you in the right direction.' Julia let Shey tag along as she made her way up to her desk and dumped her coat and bag.

'But why do you keep defining the problem as getting people to do things for you?' Julia had listened to Shey's framing of his challenge. 'Shey, you seem stuck in an erroneous belief that leadership is about delegation of tasks, about manipulating people, about controlling effort. If you insist on seeing leadership as a form of power, of a form of subjugation, you will likely continue to struggle.'

'You see,' Julia continued, 'it's not an uncommon approach in large organizations. Even there, our research continues to show that it is tolerated by people but not welcomed, enjoyed, or even terribly effective in the long run. People accept it because it's the norm. It's built into the fabric of how largely hierarchical, bureaucratic organizations work. When a choice arises, people invariably seek environments in which they can have greater freedom to work toward an overriding purpose or outcome. Being controlled and executing random tasks gets old very quickly for most people.'

'So, maybe I'm barking up the wrong tree. All I really want is to find a way to get my project moving. To do that, I need other people to help me. I need help to build it, to test it, to market it. I can do a lot of that myself, but at some stage, I need help.'

'In an organization, leaders often dispense with the contracting process. They skip over why something might be important, lazily just instructing instead. Most human beings, however, engage more deeply with an understanding of why their work might be important. It's a hugely powerful force when it's used. In large organizations though you have an imprisoned audience, an embedded set of resources who are retained to do whatever work is required. So... large organizations focus on what we call *legitimate* power... like the military... top-down order giving. People are paid to be available, to respond to requests, to execute compliantly.' Julia was enjoying the rare opportunity to help someone in the corporate world think more deeply about motivation, engagement, and meaning.

During the same 90 minutes once a week, Shey, Julia, and eventually Bob, discussed different approaches to getting his project launched. Shey had carefully described his problem as something above and beyond his day job with MGL Mania. They were quick to point out how working outside traditional corporate structures stripped you of title-based authorities.

'Yes, excellent way to think through leadership or, more to the point, being the catalyst for action... striving for a purpose. I like that you are taking this initiative, thinking about the challenges of galvanizing support for a project outside MGL Mania.' Bob was enthusiastic and asked lots of questions. 'Quite a challenge. You see if all you have is an idea, with no power to coerce or offer traditional forms of incentives, then that's a true test of your skills to build alliances, and to build relationships. You see, at its core, this always boils down to the power of the idea, the purpose. Combined with trust and belief. Belief and respect in the people you have surrounded yourself with. What's critical to this is demonstrating your own conviction, your own belief. Passion can be infectious, if it's genuine... authentic.'

Shey started to take the coaching sessions with Julia and Bob and put them straight into action. They became a valuable and insightful mirror to deconstruct his challenges and find new ways to think about things.

ဆၢ

Day 201–250: Think, think, think... do, do, do

Shey kept going back to the inventor's workshop. He was happy with the progress he was making in understanding how to design his prototype. Most of this was just him thinking through different designs, different ways to solve the engineering. It was intoxicating. And, after the coaching from Julia and Bob, he took a different approach of asking questions, developing a physical and virtual network. It seems the world was surprisingly full of software engineers willing to debate coding, as well as amateur gadget inventors, willing to give advice on designs.

'You'll need a power source 100 times more powerful than the existing lithium-ion technology,' typed Haruki. 'Plus, you need this to be wafer thin. I think your solution is to power it wirelessly. Here is a design I like. Basically, it's a super near-field wireless transfer... like how you charge your phone.'

'I'd code it via Red Hat. Yeah, there are some open-source templates, plus people are falling over themselves to play with AI models,' typed Ikaika. 'Yeah, love the idea. I'd be interested in debugging for you.'

Shey loved this collaboration process. What he didn't like was waking up each day and having to spend a growing part of each morning reconstructing how far he had progressed the previous day. However, the biggest challenge, and now obstacle, was just talking with people. There were three audiences he was splitting his time between. The engineers, they were easy. He spoke their language, and the virtual collaborations required little more than posing fascinating questions. For them it was all about the idea, the product, the gadget. But he also needed parts, supplies, materials. He had contemplated using his unique status to 'requisition' them. After all, this was for the benefit of humanity. The trouble was his claim to eminent domain didn't have any truck with authorities. So, he had to spend a portion of each day gathering parts and dealing with the associated hassle.

The third constituency he dubbed 'other people'. Try as he might, he couldn't avoid having to deal with people to help him construct, test, and manage interfaces. These people were time black holes with their constant diversions, unhelpful anecdotes, and emotional combustibility. Where he had rediscovered these last few months his love for making things, solving engineering problems, creating something, solving a problem, he had also found out just how much dealing with 'other people' was so very draining.

෪ඣ

Day 251: Adding a new dimension to Bob Challack (and Julia) – part 2

'Dealing with people is hard,' Shey confessed. 'The engineering work makes me happy, and I think I'm making progress, but when it comes to dealing with the non-engineering aspects, it doesn't come naturally to me.'

'Well, maybe you are simply trying to do too much yourself. If you're looking for me to tell you that there's a way for you to avoid dealing with "other people", I'm afraid you will be disappointed,' Julia replied.

'I quite agree,' Bob said. 'What you should do is partner up with someone who is a good balance for you. You sound like you need a natural extrovert, a gregarious relationship-focused personality. You know, we have someone who is the epitome of that profile coming today. You may know him… Emi Silva.' Bob stopped as Shey's face collapsed, and he seemed to develop a facial tic. 'Are you ok? Did you just get stung by something?'

While Shey sat silently, thinking through the implications of Bob's suggestion, Bob quietly whispered to Julia, 'You know we should look back at the tests we have been using. I think everything we've seen from Shey till now had shown him as an extroverted superhero. That's not really who he is at all.'

⁎⁎⁎

Day 252 onwards: Speculating on the contents of Pandora's box

'... and that's why I think I'm just weird. I'm missing a section of DNA. Something that other humans get at birth. Maybe I'm short of a gene.' Shey was bothering Uncle Freddy again during his walk. 'I don't look at couples, children, families and find myself envying them. The traditional path that others seem to aspire toward, or long for... desire even, I just don't feel that... pull... or urge.'

'And that's fine, Shey. I would argue that's not really the point though. The point is about finding what makes you happy. Experimenting to find pastimes, company, friendships that amplify and complement you. Don't be misled into believing that there is a formula or design that you should follow. This isn't like going to the supermarket and picking out something from the emotional fulfilment aisle.

'Try to think about this differently. It's a little clichéd but you will know it when you find it. There are emotions inside you that I know you are capable of experiencing. I suspect because societal conventions brainwash everyone into believing they should come from some template; you've told yourself that you are incapable. In my view, you've really not even scratched the surface of exploring. I strongly, strongly believe that if you try, that emotional Geiger counter inside you will start pinging. And when it does, it may surprise you with what it unleashes.'

80CZ

Day 253–300: The journey to Emi's door

As each day went by, Shey's frustrations with 'other people' increased. As much as he tried, his progress came at a cost. Not only did he find it took an increasing number of precious minutes and hours, but it was also exhausting.

'Well… there's no need to get bent out of shape about it! I'm just saying that this old Motorola razor phone is now a collector's item. I could put this on eBay and make a nice profit. If you want it, it'll cost you $200. That's almost giving it away.'

Every day he did the same dance with Harry, the owner of the electronics component and pawn store. Every day the haggle started like this and ended with Shey buying it for $50. The crazy thing was that Shey didn't care what it cost. He knew money had no meaning for him. But Harry seemed to be fonder of the dance than profit.

'OK Harry, here's $200.'

'What? No, you're supposed to negotiate. Look kid, you'll never get far in business if you just accept the first price you get quoted. Look, you now say… $25. Go on, say that.'

This daily ritual was tiresome. He had tried to source parts from different places, but this was the only place he'd been able to find the Motorola. It worked so much better than the Nokia. After this stop, he needed to get the taser, and the copper plates, and the used battery from the car salvage yard. This took at least two hours out of every morning. Two hours he could usefully spend programming and testing.

'I need help,' Shey said out loud. Harry took this as encouragement to educate Shey further on negotiation skills. Against the backdrop of Harry's sermon, Shey reflected on the suggestion that Julia and Bob had made. They have been spot-on in their coaching to this point. They are neutral, they're not clouded by knowing what went before between Emi and me. Maybe they're right. 'Anyway, what's the worst that could happen… there's always tomorrow.'

'Worst… I'll tell you worst… bankruptcy, negative cashflow… weren't you listening… who did I say was king? CASH IS KING!' Harry exclaimed.

༅༅༅

Day 301–364: Who is this Emi and what have you done with the real one?

Shey approached the apartment building. A five-storey brownstone, with half a dozen steps leading to what looked like an intercom for the apartments. It wasn't what he expected. Modest, sitting in a transitional part of town. He walked up and pressed the button saying *Silvas*.

'Go away pooh-pooh head… hahaha… heehee,' a young voice blurted.

'Carlos! No… that's not nice. Come away from there. Sorry about that,' a female voice interjected. 'How can I help you?'

'It's Shey Sinope, I was hoping to speak with Emi.' Just then Emi appeared, slightly out of breath and rather sweaty.

'Well, I never! Bom dia… Senhor Sinope. Decided to slum it over here in the less fashionable part of town? Are you lost?' Emi's face broadened to accommodate an unnaturally wide smile. 'You look so serious. *Somesing* the matter? You need to talk, estimado colega?' Emi sat on the step and beckoned Shey to join him.

It took Shey a few days to get the conversation with Emi right. The first few days, Shey managed to shoot himself in the foot. The main issue was overcoming Emi's suspicion that Shey was trying to sabotage him.

'Shey, despite what you may *sink*, I have no desire to get in your way, upset your plans, or cause you harm. But you must understand, I have fought hard to get where I am, to have a shot at senior management at MGL Mania. You haven't exactly made it easy for me. And… let's be clear… you've made it abundantly clear that you don't care for my way of working, *sim*? So… let's just say, you and I start with something of a trust deficit.'

Shey had to admit, listening to Emi didn't make him very proud of himself. Emi recounted numerous examples where Shey had repackaged and taken credit for his ideas, hung him out in presentations when he'd needed help or simply prompted him with the wrong elusive word in English; he also used humour as a weapon, to undermine and demean things Emi suggested.

'Look, I know I'm not very polished. I did not go to a top university. I did not come from a middle-class family. I learned early that if I was going to make *somesing* of myself, I would have to fight for it. So, that is what I have done. I fought to make use of every opportunity, kicked open doors, refused to allow people to say no or close me down before I'd at least a chance to prove myself. However, you see Shey, while I may not be polished, I know people. Despite having seen some terrible things in my childhood, I have always believed in the inherent goodness that exists in everyone. And that's my superpower. I love people. I come alive around *oser* people. *Seir* energy increases my energy. Sure, I need to make a living… I have a family to support, one kid about to go to school, a second on the way, and my parents, they are aging, and they rely on me. But I do love helping people, forming teams, suggesting solutions. I have thousands of ideas. The more people I interact with the more possibilities appear to me. The spark of collaboration… *tudo bem*. But my ideas are gifts, for people who I trust, to use. The only request I make is that we share in any success that follows.'

As Shey took the time, the successive days to understand Emi better, Shey began to see him in a new light.

'Well… I see how that might have appeared… but let me assure you Emi… it wasn't that I was deliberately being not nice.' These attempts were obviously rejected. Emi was due to attend the final day of the assessment. There was no way he would give that up for something less than a miracle.

And then something of a miracle occurred.

'You know, Emi, I think you may be a better senior executive for MGL Mania than me. You have a passion and conviction that I can't say I feel. For me, the job at MGL Mania was a surrogate and crutch, to make me feel good about myself. I think I've found something more important to do.' Shey looked up at the open window above and the faces beckoning to Emi that it was time for him to get ready for his big day. 'Perhaps I can help you. Brainstorm today's assessments with you. And if you feel willing, we can meet at lunch or after you finish, and you can maybe coach me on how to be better at dealing with people.'

Over the next few weeks, Shey and Emi spent many hours together. They discussed not only where they were different, but also where they were the same. Shey shared his big idea. Emi loved it and suggested a hundred ways it could be improved. Shey shared the big obstacles he was facing in making a prototype. Emi suggested a multitude of ways to overcome them.

৪৩৪৪

Evening 365: Now it's open... there's no putting things back!

'… and it was tough. But the Gautam Buddha fast was enlightening.' Shey was recounting his quest to find the real Shey Sinope over dinner. His version of *Eat, Pray, Love* was more extreme and included legendary fasts and obscure quests. 'It provided me with a deep sense of tranquillity, a connection deep inside. Of all the transcendental, mystic journeys I have tried, it was more substantive than the audience with the Dalai Lama, gave me more answers than the FaceTime with the Pope, and made more sense to me than the pursuit of the Samma-samadhi.'

'How interesting. I have some friends who fast for Yom Kippur. Eventually the side effects… *Passover.*' Shey's dinner companion shared his sense of humour. It was one of the many things he liked about their company. 'Did you find answers? The Pandora's box you mention. What did you find inside?'

'People typically find purpose or identity through responsibility to a family or a deep conviction around work. Some find answers to who they are in their heritage or their ancestry. Others, like elite athletes or research scientists, are driven by the dream of achieving a goal or lab result. Others have an unshakeable spiritual faith. The one thing I thought I knew was that I was spectacularly average at everything. It can be very tiresome, failing, losing, and feeling inadequate. So, I found a way to feel better about myself. Trouble is it was all fake. And then I got trapped by pretending. The more I did it, the longer I persevered, the harder it became to admit it wasn't really making me happy. I told myself it was because I hadn't reached my destination. I saw how others reacted to my work achievements at MGL Mania. They seemed impressed, even a bit jealous. I assumed sooner or later, with perhaps the next promotion, or the next pay raise, something would click.

'The truth is it never did. Each promotion, each pay raise, if anything, proved less fulfilling. Each moment of satisfaction was more fleeting, more fake. My problem, I have come to understand, is that I spent far too much of my time being blown and buffeted by the winds of others' expectations. Of how I believed people expected me to act or expected me to behave. I never felt any deep connection with people, spirituality, or work because I was approaching it all from fundamentally the wrong perspective. I've finally, I think, figured out that measuring myself, basing my identity and outlook on what I perceive others expect of me, well, it just doesn't work, it's a mirage, a façade, what are they called... like those Russian villages… Potemkin… I had constructed some fake village to live in.[1]

'You want to know what I found when I opened what I call my Pandora's box? I pictured it as a room inside myself that I had closed and shuttered in my teens. Something I had abandoned, dismissing it as a weakness, a disability. Basically, I was afraid of what might be inside that room. Some terrible darkness. Something deformed. Something inhuman…

'Say… what time do you go on stage? Don't we need to head over to the theatre?'

'Sashay, that's such a tease. It's a little after 9pm. I'm due on stage at…' Before Babs could finish, they were accosted by an exuberant Shey Sinope. 'Stop, stop… you'll smudge my make up.'

Shey jumped up and down and danced around. He hugged Babs as tightly as he could and gave them a huge kiss. 'It's after 9pm… it's after 9pm… I'm not a pumpkin… there is no rowdy crowd… no electrical storm…' In his excitement he checked his watch. In a reflex, perhaps brought on by a year of muscle memory… he pressed the red button.

Beep-beep-beep… beep-beep-beep…

'Shoot… why did I do that?'

Chapter 6

The first day of the rest of your life – TGI Friday!

'♩♫♫♩♩♫♫♩♫♫'...

What a sweet sound. Shey had long ago stopped checking the calendar, his phone, even searching for the latest news. What was the point? However, in recent days it was less the futility of the exercise and more the genuine excitement about what lay ahead.

He jumped out of bed. There was a time for contemplative silence. A time for quiet reflection. But Shey felt music was always there. Even in its absence, there was still a soundtrack. The ambient noise of the room, the pervasive beat of the traffic down below. Sometimes music created a mood, but today, he needed something to accompany how he felt. He knew exactly what today needed.

Elbow had written the perfect song. He marvelled at the amazing sound of Guy's voice. He sang along and swished open his window blinds. The sunlight flooded the room. He danced with unusual abandon. Shey felt invigorated, refreshed, hopeful. He paused, closed his eyes, and took a deep breath. Sightlessly, he embraced the beauty around him. Lots to be thankful for, lots to look forward to. Time to make every moment count.

He didn't take long to get ready. He dressed in a simple *Chirimoya* t-shirt and jeans. Something that just felt comfortable and fitted his frame of mind. He grabbed a pair of bright sneakers from his wardrobe. And a beanie, mainly to hide his somewhat unkempt hair. He headed out to start his day, humming as he went.

৪০৫৪

'So, it's *FRIDAY*!… IT IS FRIDAY!!!!' Ellen sat across from Shey in her local coffee shop spot. 'For some reason I thought you'd be doing cartwheels… wearing a silly grin… or holding up a big sign. How did you figure it out? How did you break the cycle? How long did it take? What was the secret… Tell me… TELL ME!'

'It is?'

'What… that's it? Shey Sinope… SHEY,' Ellen realized people were looking and took it down a notch. 'Mister… come on… explanation… now!'

Shey admired his friend. She was literarily jumping out of her chair. He, on the other hand, was feeling strangely calm. His thoughts churned a little across everything that had happened: his unhealthy fixation with FAB, his paranoia to escape his time bubble, and now, well, a sort of contentment, almost Zen like.

'Ellen, I get it. And let me assure you, this hasn't been some big practical joke… at least not with you as the victim.' Shey wondered why he wasn't more excited, more exuberant. 'The honest answer is that as much as breaking the time loop is a big relief, I find myself with mixed feelings. And that in itself probably tells you a lot about how my outlook has changed over the past… well… year. If there was some key, obviously I must have found it. But I'll be damned if I could tell you what it was. It's as much a mystery to me as how the whole thing began.'

Shey looked over at Ellen and saw she wasn't entirely convinced.

'Ellen, here's what I know for sure. Today, when I woke, I was happy. I was looking forward to my day. I think the main difference between me a year ago and the me you see today is that I've figured a few things out. Probably, if I was going to point to the single biggest change, it's that I've let some things go. Some things that were probably holding me back, weighing me down. But I've also embraced some new things, things that I think I was previously scared of, or blind to. I've got an intriguing work project that is inspiring me. Plus, after a lot of trepidation, I've found some other things that make me happy. Things I believe that are mine, where I've been able to separate my desire to please and conform, and instead listen more carefully to my own emotions.' Shey drifted off. 'You know I must tell you about what I saw during my Gautam Buddha fast.'

'It still puzzles me why you aren't jumping for joy. Repeating the same day couldn't have been a lot of fun. Now, well, the world is your oyster again…' Ellen said with a slight shake of her head.

'Ah… you know there may be something in that! I think I had become very good at the whole rinse, dunk, repeat cycle. Now, well, life will become a lot less predictable. Yes, the hocus pocus may stop, but all the chaos and calamity of life will begin again.' Shey thought out loud. 'However, enough of that for now. At least I'm in better shape to take on the absurdity of professional life now. But all this reminds me I am forgetting something important. I promised myself that if the spell was ever broken, I would fish out my list of atonements, requests for forgiveness, and simple apologies. Ahhh… here it is. Now item #1 seems apt, and I should begin immediately.' Shey paused, looked Ellen in the eye. 'Ellen Elpis, let me apologize for all the times I wasn't a great friend to you, let me thank you for all of your belief and willingness to stick with me, and… finally… let me solemnly swear, I will evermore have your back.'

'I'm honoured and humbled… but no apology is necessary. I'm still trying to come to terms with yesterday's whole Nostradamus thing.[1] It spooked me. Don't get me wrong, I don't doubt you, or what happened. It's just… well, a bit out there. I can't imagine how terrible it must have been to live the same day over and over again.' Ellen shuddered at the thought.

'I had some tough days for sure. Some dark thoughts. Mainly in the beginning. I went through denial, grief, anger, and I had a very long period of indulgent wound licking. In the end though, I realized I had a simple choice, feel sorry for myself, be angry at the world and my predicament, or make the best of it. In the end, it was ok. Actually, in some ways, it felt a little bit like a superpower.' Shey had a flashback to his crazy FAB bungled burglary attempt.

'That sort of leads me to my next item on my long atonement list. You may remember a couple weeks back in your time, before the groundhog craziness, I bragged to you I had figured out a foolproof way to beat the career game. The napkin formula? I know you didn't buy it… but I did. I now realize the whole formula thing was madness. Me trying to make a science out of a game that wasn't even worth playing. I was so desperate to be good at something, to win at a game so many other people seemed to think was important. It became something of an obsession.' Shey saw Ellen nodding in agreement. 'I took the whole game-theory concept and applied it to my work at MGL Mania. Like a career version of mortgage-backed security valuation models or trying to reduce human behaviour to something like rock, paper, scissors,' Shey said with a wry grin. 'I really do look back now and think how silly it all was. But for a while… you know… I did think I'd cracked the code. There was something about it that worked. Something that got me noticed.'

'Well, Shey Sinope… you have changed! How far does this new self-awareness go I wonder? Is it just the euphoria of escaping an endless sea of Thursdays? You need to be careful you don't strain a muscle. You know if you keep this up you might be in some serious trouble… people might enjoy spending time with you!'

'OK… yes… I deserve that. I am willing to concede that if we repeat this day a thousand more times, I will still have deserved it.' Catching himself, he continued, 'You know the funny thing about how my brain works? Even after realizing my mistake, I still found myself trying to explain where I was going wrong by creating a new, simpler, formula.'

$$Life = \int_{Death}^{Birth} \frac{happiness}{time} \times \textit{Happiness and Time}$$

$$\textit{(First, do no harm!)}$$

Shey pointed to the scribble on his napkin.

'You can't do much about your birth and death… putting aside arguments of healthy living and such. These are the two fixed points. But as far as I can see it, the rest of life is a factor of how much happiness you can achieve over time. The caveat though, the Big Kahuna that is easy to overlook, is that it all has to mean something… be for something good… a purpose greater than just selfish indulgence. Certainly, the whole "first cause no harm" label should apply to us all.' He screwed the napkin up and threw it in the nearest recycling. 'Of course, it's rubbish, just like the first formula. I know that now. I think I knew it back when I first showed you my corporate game-theory cheat formula. Leading a good, fulfilling, happy life is too complex, too dynamic, too unpredictable, well… just too chaotic. You must start by believing in yourself, you have to believe in something. That was my biggest problem. I simply didn't have a deep conviction… about anything really. Apart perhaps from our friendship… my family… and maybe one other person who I met this… year of Thursdays.'

'I sense you really mean all of that. I must say I'm very pleased you've dispensed with that silly career ladder formula. I never really understood why it was all so important to you.'

'Changing the subject, slightly, I wonder what you're doing later. I'd like you to come to dinner with a couple of friends. I think you'll like them.'

ಬಂಚ

'Ah… Mr Sinope… we meet again, *sim*?' Emi greeted Shey with his trademark grin. 'The day, yesterday, went exactly as you predicted. I think I did *boa*.'

'Good. I'm glad. Happy it helped.' Shey had caught up with Emi in the office.

'You, look, how do they say over here, relaxed? I've never understood that observation, on the face of it, it sounds like a compliment. However, I detect it really means something less complimentary, like lazy or complacent or dishevelled.' Emi looked at Shey's appearance. 'So, you are now starting an "attending-a-rock-concert-casual-business-attire" trend, blurring the boundaries. I like it!'

'I meant what I told you, Emi. I'm done with conforming to meaningless rules and regulations. I'm not exactly going to streak around the office naked… but I don't see the need for dressing in a corporate uniform, for no good reason. Let's see what happens. I doubt they'd fire me for it… but I'm not going to play the corporate soldier game anymore. Anyhow, that's beside the point… I just wanted to see how you are doing and maybe see if I could persuade you to do a little moonlighting?'

'Beleza, por que… but tell me… how is your *FEEL VR* project?'

'Yes, I think I have a working prototype. I was hoping I could persuade you to join me in making the pitch next week. The angel investors you suggested, they seem interested. But I'm not confident doing it on my own.[2] I'd like you there to partner with me. I'm hoping to twist one other person's arm to join us. Would you consider it?'

'Well… let me think about it. I have some time this weekend. Maybe you can show me how far you've got. That will give me a better idea of what I might be able to do to help. One caveat amigo… I need to prioritize MGL Mania. If I help, it has to be on understanding that my MGL Mania commitments take precedence.'

'Sure… completely understand. I'm planning a little informal get-together this evening. Maybe I could persuade you to join us? I can introduce you to the *FEEL VR* voluntary task force. I think you'll like them. Either way… free drinks?'

'OK… let me confirm after seeing what the family is up to. I hope to see you this evening, Senhor Sinope.'

੪୭ଔ

Shey spent a few hours in the office looking at his email, talking to colleagues about the status of some projects. In many cases, the projects seemed different to how he remembered them. It wasn't only that he felt like he'd been away a year. No, some of the projects seemed more pointless than he remembered them. In a couple of cases, there really didn't seem to be any obvious outcomes.

He thought about whether it was worth cutting back some activity. Was it all necessary? Were they worth the time and cost? He'd need to give it some more thought. His office phone rang. He was momentarily startled. He didn't even remember he had an office phone.

'Mr Sinope, oh good, I've finally reached you. This is Ralph Canine's office calling.' Shey smiled at the thought of Ralph's office calling. 'Mr Canine wondered if you could meet with him today, at 3pm?' It was apparent this wasn't really a request, perhaps not even an expectation… the phone went dead almost before Shey had muttered an 'OK'.

∞☻∞

There was a momentary hesitation as Ralph saw Shey at the entrance to his office.

'Errr… Chey… I wasn't aware you were off today. Did you come in especially for this meeting?'

'You have no need to be concerned, Ralph. Everything will be OK.' Shey felt completely calm. He thought about his earlier self that had longed for this moment. The anointment meeting. Being asked to visit Ralph was typically for only two reasons… some big promotion or appointment… or the reverse. He knew which of the two this was likely to be.

'Ahh… well… OK. Well, why don't you take a…' Ralph turned to find Shey had already seated. 'Yes… good.' Ralph picked up some papers from his desk and walked over to the small conference table. 'Did something happen to your regular work clothes? Perhaps a spillage or something?'

Shey was aware of Ralph's strange discomfort at his appearance. He took a slight pang of pleasure from it. All too often when you get called in to a senior executive's office the balance of power is tilted. It's like the environment had been designed to intimidate, to put the visitor on the defensive. He liked how his lack of thought and completely instinctive decision to wear ordinary clothes had this disorientating effect on Ralph.

And why should it matter? He really didn't know. Most start-up companies had long ago figured out that letting people make their own decisions about how they dressed was a smart thing to do. Controlling, legislating for appearance is such a strange thing when you think about it. It either means you don't trust people to make reasonable decisions about what they wear to work, or you have some stick up your butt about imposing your own views, and hang-ups, on others. *When FEEL VR has employees… they'll be able to be whoever they want to be…. wear whatever they want,* he resolved.

'What is it you would like to talk about?' Shey tried to move things along. He knew why he was here. He'd experienced it so many times over the last year it was no longer something that he really thought about. In fact, this was the first time he had given it any thought in months.

In that moment, he realized it didn't matter to him anymore. All the energy, all the planning, all the anxiety. The loss of sleep, the nervous evenings alone stressing about what might go wrong, how to increase his chances of winning. He remembered just how much effort he had put into the CAPs programme. He shook his head as he remembered how he had built it up to be so important. The crowning glory of his career to this point.

'I wanted to talk to you about the CAPs assessment centre. Did you get my email last night?'

'Actually, no, I'm sorry, I didn't.' His Thursday routine was far too busy with other things to read it last night. And today. Why didn't he look at the email in his inbox? That was strange. He remembered seeing it. He had just skipped over it. That was a decent clue that it no longer had a control over him.

'Well, that's unfortunate. You see I understand you didn't attend the last full last day of the assessment. We tried to contact you but were unsuccessful. What happened?'

'Yesterday was an extraordinary day, Ralph. Let's just say that I gave the assessment process everything I had. In the end, I realized that the best thing for me, and MGL Mania, was not to waste too much of everyone's time. I did have a very good conversation with Bob and Julia about this. I think they understood.'

'Ah-hah… well, you do understand how expensive it is for us to invest in these assessment centres? And how sought-after the places are?'

'Let me assure you, Ralph, that I don't think anyone has ever taken the CAPs assessment programme more seriously than me.'

'Well… taking everything into account, and in particular having discussed your case with Bob in some considerable detail…' Shey started to tune out a little as Ralph recounted the assessment process. He was saying something about how the programme was designed to provide only a minimum assurance on the basic intellectual, critical thinking, and drive components of each participant. He then started talking about emotional intelligence, and how MGL Mania had been working hard to break the difficult cycle of appointing leaders who were mirror images of incumbents. He mentioned something about Level 5 leaders, about authenticity, about self-awareness, about 'activists' and 'intre-preneurship.' Ralph seemed to be on a soap box... his voice was raising in volume and his eyes seemed to widen. Apparently, Ralph really did believe whatever the CAPs programme was doing was critical if MGL Mania were going to remain relevant in the coming years.

Shey was thinking about something else. Did he want to continue to work at MGL Mania? The main issue for Shey was one of pragmatism. He really wanted to see what would happen with the *FEEL VR* set. He was excited about that. The work he had been doing didn't feel like work... at least not the way it did at MGL Mania. He could see a purpose, a very real outcome. And... it was fun to work on something like a very big version of his childhood models. Something that combined his love of invention with building something and learning some cool things about AI programming. Plus, he had managed to get help with the aspects that he didn't enjoy quite as much. He saw Ellen and Emi as the perfect balance to him; their instincts were much better attuned to the community. Emi amazed Shey in just how people seemed to warm to him, to see him as almost instinctively someone good to be around. Emi's energy seemed to create an aura and anyone in close proximity seemed to feel better about themselves, about work, about life. It was an amazing thing to see.

But… he needed somewhere to live. Needed to pay some bills. Needed to fund his new venture. He hoped that they might get some investment in the coming weeks. Something that might both validate but also partially fund the prototype development. Shey struggled with the idea of just abruptly leaving MGL Mania. That didn't seem right either.

'… and so that's why we've decided that we want you to join the CAPs programme.'

'Wait… *say what now?*' Shey felt certain he had misheard Ralph.

'Yes, Bob and the FAB team were unanimous… you are exactly what we need. Not afraid to break with convention, willing to walk your own path, and self-aware enough to know when you need help. I must say… I was also a bit surprised… but we trust FAB's process.' Ralph passed Shey a bundle of CAP's swag. 'Here is the welcome pack, including of course….' Ralph picked out a horrible bright yellow baseball hat, '…the famous CAPs CAP!'

Shey was stunned.

'Ralph… is it OK if I think about this? Maybe I can take the weekend?'

'Yes, Chey, why don't you take the weekend. It would be a bit unprecedented, but if you feel you'd rather not take your place on the programme… well… you certainly don't have to.'

80CB

Shey left the office earlier than normal. No need to be there any longer than necessary. And he had some things to think about. There was the day at the office, again, after a long while. Some people he hadn't seen for a long while… who of course thought it strange when Shey greeted them with effusive hugs and questions of how they were doing after all this time.

There was the work itself. Generally, Shey thought some of the work at MGL Mania could be interesting. He looked at it very differently today than a… year ago. Now, he looked more deeply into the projects, the substance, the intended outcomes. If you filtered out the pretentiousness and looked at the core… well, there were some things in there that had merit.

The trouble was it came with some, well, BS. He did a little inventory of the things in his inbox, calendar, and discussions he had had. He guessed about 50% didn't have much purpose or substance. The vestiges of well-intended initiatives that had spiralled into banality. In some cases, he noted with a self-effacing mental wink, these were projects he had volunteered for because they gave him access, or some perceived political advantage.

But these weren't the big things from the day. There was the surprising twist on the whole CAPs admission, and, of course, the very fact that it was FRIDAY! A constant background thought throughout his day had been the progress he had made to understand himself, to reacquaint himself with the real Shey Sinope. *Ultimately, I think this is the key to deciding what I should do, where I spend my time, what I should prioritize,* he thought. He decided to walk rather than take the train.

ಐಾಯ

'Uncle, how are you doin' today?'

'Well, Shey, two consecutive days. Admit it… I am your favourite uncle.'

'You are my only uncle!' Shey had spoken with his uncle most days over the last year. 'So, I've been thinking a lot about the story you told me about the coffee and the cups. It occurs to me that it could have multiple meanings.'

'Well, if it stuck with you and made you think, that's a good start.'

'The story literally highlights the apparent superficiality of the students, right? The proxy is that the cups represent appearance, and the contents represent substance. A form-over-function parable? On this level then, the story asks the listener to reflect on whether they are living a superficial life. Whether they are prioritizing how things look rather than what they do, how they feel, how they taste.'

'I sense you're not finished.'

'I've thought a lot about this. It's really hard not to get swept along with the prevailing wisdom, and the collective convention of what is desirable. I've come to think of this as the consumerism principle of scarcity increasing desirability. The question here seems to be whether you are content being swayed by the crowd… by pursuing something simply because others think it's valuable.'

'Interesting. You may want to take a little break. This thinking is probably exhausting you.'

'I haven't quite finished.' Shey was using the call with his uncle to sort through his thoughts. They were still a little jumbled. The thought of his uncle listening helped him make sense of them... put them in some kind of order. 'I've tried a lot of things to better understand myself. To reconnect with the real Shey Sinope. Treks, quests, meditation. Even tried that Gautam Buddha fast you mentioned. Well, I completed it. Guess what I saw at the end of the 49 days?'

'And what was that?'

'Two cups of coffee. That was it. Just two cups of coffee. One was a beautiful ceramic design. The other a horribly amateurish pottery project. I picked each up... sipped from their contents.'

'... and?'

'Well... that was it. I had arranged an Uber Eats delivery and I woke to the smell of lukewarm pizza.' Shey paused before continuing. 'I'm now figuring out what it symbolized. Connecting some dots. It helped me see something... something deeper. It explains why I have not found or even sought romantic connections. I had a huge blind spot. Something stopping me from really seeing. The world seems preoccupied by labels, by shapes, sizes, and promotes curated forms of beauty... and assigns them desirability. Until recently, I found separating the cup from its contents impossible. It was just easier to pretend that I wasn't interested in any of it. Since I couldn't get excited by the things most other people did... well, you just assume you must be missing something.

'If I were to say to you that I think I can love the contents of the cup but find the container confusing, does that make any sense to you?'

'Perfectly Shey!' Uncle Freddy's voice cracked a little as he spoke.

ꙮ

'Thanks guys…' Shey sat at the restaurant booth. 'This is a dream come true. Not just because it's Friday, not just because it's after 9pm, not even because it's not storming outside…'

'Shey, Shey Sinope… I thought that was you. Hey everyone come over here. It's Shey!' The man looked like he had been partying hard for the last 24 hours. 'See… I told you it was him.' He shouted at one of his well-worn group of friends. 'And look…. it's Babs the Barista too! So cool.'

Six familiar, if less rowdy, people crowded around Shey's table.

'Look, we want to thank you. Things could have gotten a bit out of hand yesterday. This bachelor weekend started early for us and well… we didn't exactly wear it well. You made our first night in the big city amazing. Babs… you are hilarious. And Shey, you didn't need to hook us up with the hotel and transport. How can we ever repay you?'

'No problem. Happy to help. I'm pleased you stayed out of trouble… well at least didn't get arrested.' The group laughed unnecessarily loudly. They migrated away, shouting Shey compliments and repeating their thanks.

'Who were they?' asked Ellen.

'Long story… but a group of revellers who I've bumped into a few times over the past year.' Shey responded. He was about to continue when he was distracted by another set of interlopers.

'Shey Ssss… Sinope… you are a legend at Fffff… FAB!' Bob seemed like he was also having a good evening. He slurred a couple of his words. Julia appeared to be trying to shepherd him towards an awaiting taxi. 'Love your work. Loved spending time with you these last few days. Honestly, it's made a late middle-aged… somewhat cynical… old industrial psychologist… eufffourkick… youforkic…'

'He's had a good week. My apologies for his uncharacteristic lack of eloquence. He doesn't usually drink but insisted we came out this evening. Said he wanted to let what's left of his hair down… something about taking a page out of your book,' Julia said apologetically.

'And where else would you be tonight of all nights… TGIF! I told Shey that he ran the risk of bumping into a few familiar faces tonight. He's told everyone over the past… well, little while… that if he ever saw another Friday… this is where he'd be.' Babs looked at Shey and shook their head, smiling.

'Julia, Bob… thanks for all your advice and wisdom. I can assure you, whatever little I may have left you with, you have made an exponentially bigger impact on me. I can't thank you enough! And… yes… as promised… RING THE BELL BARTENDER… THE NEXT ROUND IS ON ME!'

After the mayhem of the next 10 or 15 minutes subsided, Shey turned back to his dining party.

'A toast to all of you. To Emi, Ellen, Babs… thank you for believing in me, thank you for trusting me, thank you for taking an incredible leap of faith to help me navigate this… extraordinary thing. I still can't believe it's Friday. But beyond that… thank you for choosing to be in my life!'

They clinked glasses.

'I have a burning *question*. What happens next?' Emi asked.

'Beyond building *FEEL VR*? Beyond deciding when, rather than if, I move on from MGL Mania? Obviously, I plan to decline the CAPs membership. It would be wrong to do that and potentially steal the place from someone else. But I suspect you mean the more important stuff… right?

'Well, first, I plan on going on a first date.' He paused looking at them each and lingering on Babs. 'Then there are so many things... I'd like to stay awake all night, watch the sunset... and wait for the sunrise. I'd like to watch leaves turn orange and gold, then fall to the ground. Feel the heat and the cold, the full beauty of the seasons. I want to swim in every ocean, visit every continent. Experience the great wonders of the modern world. I'd like to plant a garden, and watch it grow. Grow a beard... and then shave it off. Make some plans, watch the calendar count down, and feel what it's like for them to become a memory. I want to be physically present for every birthday, anniversary, christening, and major milestone for people I care about... and be unnecessarily generous in my gift giving.' Shey looked around the table, catching each of their stares. 'But above all, I want to have conversations, experiences, and overcome challenges with each of you.'

PART II
LIVING PROFESSIONAL LIFE
ON YOUR OWN TERMS

Chapter 7

A groundhog career – introduction to Part II

A *Groundhog Career* explores what we believe are the big 'intrinsic' questions we often subconsciously suppress in our 20s and 30s. And let's be clear, it's completely understandable to banish thoughts of identity, happiness, fulfilment, purpose, and collateral damage while you are establishing your early career. You are busy focusing on navigating a perilous new chapter in your life. Business, corporations, employers, and investors can be very intimidating. It's entirely natural to focus on trying to be who you think they want you to be and approaching your career as a competition, not of your making, where there appear to be winners and losers… and you want to be a winner. This takes a lot of effort. Perhaps even all your cognitive processing power. The problem, however, is the reality is something different. It's hard to recognize them, but you are likely being swept along by the influence of powerful invisible forces. Forces that you unconsciously adopt and wear as a cloak. Willingly, even enthusiastically. Most of us want to belong, want to feel included, want to be among the 'cool' kids. Ironically, sometimes that desire to belong leads us to ride roughshod over colleagues. In the process, we suppress or postpone exploring deeper questions about who we are, what we need, and how our personal desires, goals, and aspirations might languish.

Have you found yourself, perhaps late at night, trying to quiet your mind before sleep, but elusive thoughts, ill-defined feelings of doubt, or insecurity, keep bouncing around your head? Have you compared yourself to others and asked questions about not just whether they have more than you, but whether they seem happier than you? Do you admire and perhaps gravitate toward people who seem certain they know who they are? Do you find yourself adopting some of these same people's views and opinions? Have you played games and had fantasies about what you would do if you won the lottery, or suddenly came into a lot of money? Do those dreams involve escaping your current existence and being/doing something else?

While the world of jobs, the spectrum of career opportunities, seems to be fast evolving, the questions of identity, purpose, and meaning, are more eternal. We make the case that the majority of so-called career advice focuses on navigating the job acquisition process and on maximizing the return on your efforts. Few of them provide guidance on the more dangerous perils of losing sight of the qualitative aspects of professional life. Even 'work-life balance' books do not really address these deeper questions. They focus more on the time management aspects of personal and professional life.

Our need for meaning, fulfilment, and purpose is much deeper and more vital to our wellbeing. Plato, for example, encouraged us to think of the purpose of life as pursuing wisdom and understanding.[1] He believed that the human soul must be fed to be fulfilled and its sustenance was knowledge gained through the furtherance of our community, society, or even more grandly, humanity. More contemporary philosophers such as Martin Heidegger and William James reinforced this theme by pointing to our need for personal authenticity and holding a core belief that we are in pursuit of something profoundly worthwhile.[2,3]

Many of us have learned about Abraham Maslow, the father of humanistic psychology, and his hierarchy of needs which we briefly referred to earlier.[4] In the 75 years since he published his work, successive generations of psychologists have added to and reinforced his central tenet. Human beings have a deep need to find personal meaning. To understand how our efforts make sense in a holistic sense. In short, working solely for financial or other 'hygiene' factors as Herzberg described them, doesn't sustain us.[5]

We ignore this core human need at our peril. When we fall into the trap of confusing the means with the ends, the journey for the destination, the symptoms for the disease, we lose a vital ingredient in finding and sustaining happiness. Material success without spiritual meaning and purpose is superficial, a shiny façade that hides a troubling darkness. For most of us, this does sound intuitively right. In the quiet moments, when we allow ourselves to put aside the burden we carry, we sense the need for something substantive to centre us.

But, to dispel any doubts, in the following pages we will reinforce the lessons embedded in Shey's story by walking through the *career game trap, the identity confusion paradox* as well as exploring how *leadership* can easily be misused and perverted in the process. Shey's story is designed to illustrate the emptiness that accompanies *getting what you wanted only to find it's not what you needed.*

The core of this book is about finding lasting career fulfilment and living a professional life on your own terms. This requires us to be confident and content with answering the deceptively complex questions: 'Why am I doing this?' and 'What is this ultimately all for?' Alongside this essential challenge, we explain the powerful forces that distract and confuse us. Society, family, friends, the job market, are pushing us down a road that tends to prioritize and celebrate superficial rewards. These seduce us because they are easier, simpler, more obvious. Equally, they allow us to avoid looking within ourselves, which is something few of us enjoy. Most of us would rather look outward for our validation and sense of identity. We aspire to be more like people we admire or believe that society values and celebrates. In part, this is fuelled by a sense that we are somehow empty vessels or that our hidden identities are in some way inadequate or ugly. When you think about this, it is both true and completely irrational. Our view of these idealized personalities is distorted by 'social photoshopping' and projections we ourselves superimpose on them. What idyllic lives they must have, we think. For them, the grass is truly always greener. Of course, this is not the reality! Everyone is flawed, a work in progress, occasionally uncertain and insecure, and certainly at times frustrated and unhappy.

So, a preoccupation with looking outward for validation, recognition, and identity, distracts us and misleads us. It takes us ironically further away from happiness, fulfilment, and meaning. Rather than feel worthy, we generally feel more and more inadequate by comparison to our visions of the outside world.

The trick is not to give up or ignore looking within. The way to lasting fulfilment in our professional lives is to take the time to understand ourselves, find our own meaning, and feel confident that we are investing our time in something that makes sense to us. Part of the solution is often finding something we have a deep belief in, something that transcends our own selfish needs... a cause or purpose. This is at its most powerful when it becomes a shared cause... something we also argue is a better definition of leadership than a job title.

All the evidence from Plato to Maslow, and from flower power to great resignation, reinforces that these questions never go away. They are always there in the background, nagging away at us. The longer we postpone acknowledging them, exploring them, understanding them, and setting a course to reconcile ourselves with them, ultimately the more our dissatisfaction and disillusionment will grow. This is what fuels the paradox of finding superficial success while being, increasingly, miserable.

A groundhog career - explanation

In *A Groundhog Career*, we have written a book that deals with this Janus challenge. In Part I, we shared the story of Shey Sinope struggling with understanding why he is doing what he's doing. We hope you enjoyed Shey Sinope's sequel story. Using the *living the same day until you get it right* format, we felt it worked well to explore this subject. We took Shey on a voyage from superficial, insular, career-maximizing arrogance, and confronted him with the absurdity of where that leads. In the process, we had the opportunity to explore some correlated subjects that are also close to our hearts.

In a *career game* sense, we wanted to talk about the idea of an actual (rather than metaphorical) formula for success. This is not a huge stretch of imagination, and we have known people throughout our careers who have constructed their versions of a formula. The reason it isn't a huge stretch is that companies do create systems that can be 'gamed'. Indeed, in some cases, you hear people actually say things like 'you just need to play the game', or 'this is how things really get done around here'. All companies have systems for pay reviews, promotions, bonuses, and more general recognition. Enormous effort is invested to maintain these systems and upgrade the technology platforms that support them. In some instances, companies get very evangelical about them and confuse them with much more important things like outcomes, purpose, customers/people, consequences, and value creation.

Early in the story, we show Shey enjoying the superficial aspects that flow from the revelation that he is good at 'the career game'. He covets and clings to this success, feeling comforted by what he believes is the admiration, respect, and envy of those around him. It was important to show how our need to please others is such a strong influence.

We also got to show how this singular pursuit creates collateral damage. While Shey's story is fictional, the outcome of attempting to bend and shortcut for personal gain creates strange and often absurd results. The two main components of this are Shey's painting of colleagues as obstacles and pawns in his game, along with his attempts to 'hack' the promotion system. The illustrations in our story are not far from the truth. We wanted to show how we can justify this to ourselves while also showing the impact it has on those caught in its twisted web.

As our story unfolds, Shey is confronted with a problem. He is stuck. This is a metaphor for having reached the maximum limit for which his current tactics will take him. His approach has reached its capacity and unless he reinvents himself, he will be stuck forever repeating the same empty game. This is where we begin to explore what might unlock Shey and allow him to progress with the rest of his life.

The remainder of our fable follows Shey as he is forced to look in the place he fears the most. Within himself. We are all our own harshest critics. Ultimately, we know how superficial, self-centred, selfish, and cruel we can be. This can result in self-loathing and avoidance. It is easier to be the person others want you to be or adopt an identity that you think will be popular.

Shey's story illustrates his journey to get comfortable with who he really is by separating his own desires from those he believes others expect of him and start to identify what really makes him happy. It is hard to build a successful life without first establishing a core foundation. We follow Shey through a series of farcical events that lead to him exploring hidden dimensions of life, of relationships, of purpose, and we get some insights on how this influences his perceptions of identity, value, and happiness.

A groundhog career – Part II format

As advertised, Part II of this book is designed to appeal to left-brain thinking. This said, we recommit to our aims of being relevant, practical, and engaging (if not as entertaining). *A Groundhog Career* now segues into an exploration of the dual challenges we've illustrated, how you can understand and identify the risk in your career, and ways you can plot a course to a more fulfilling, sustainable, and rewarding professional journey.

We have laid out the rest of Part II as follows:

1. **Don't become a captive of the career game**. In this chapter, we look more closely at our natural tendency to look for hacks or shortcuts in professional life and the consequences if we take this too far.

2. **Pursue your career… not someone else's.** Here we look at the challenge of breaking free from the trap of measuring success purely by external measures. We explain why it is difficult but ultimately critical to look within for sources of fulfilment and satisfaction.

3. **Reframing leadership from status to shared purpose**. It's very easy for us to think of leadership as something bestowed by hierarchical promotion or business card title. We seek to challenge this thinking and to point to how it is much healthier to think of leadership as a shared cause that transcends status, title, or delegations of job tasks.

4. **And finally… in defence of formulas**. Bringing it all together and summarizing the main takeaways.

We start each of these chapters by sharing real career stories from some exceptional people. These stories highlight a component of career game playing, finding your deeper purpose, or redefining leadership. We are indebted to our contributors for sharing their real-life experiences. In our view, they bring an important extra dimension to the book, one that emphasizes actual lived experience. It is our hope that they help underline that we all face similar challenges in our professional lives, and we have the power not only to prevail but to find sustaining professional fulfilment.

Following the case studies, we share a summary of the scientific background on each subject before providing a distillation of the lessons we can learn. Each chapter closes with some thinking and reflection exercises, along with blink summaries that capture the main points for easy review and future reference.

Trisha Conley
Executive Vice President, People and Culture, LyondellBasell

It was by accident that Trisha found her way into the world of HR. 'When I started my first job, I realized that no one was providing HR support locally, so I just decided I'd do it!'

She didn't over-analyze what happened next. She saw opportunities to progress up the corporate hierarchy and took them. 'I needed to be self-sufficient. My childhood taught me tough lessons about not being dependent on anyone but myself. It was a huge driving force.'

She discovered a flair for understanding what people needed to do their jobs effectively, which led to an opportunity to join a multi-national oil company. 'I was always looking to expand boundaries and play a bigger role. Once I had the launchpad, I just put my head down and did the work. I was focused and disciplined.'

Over the next 30 years, Trisha has emerged as one of the world's leading Chief HR Officers.

Navigating adversity is part of the journey

When Trisha reflects on her career, she points out sometimes it's the setbacks that define you. 'I don't believe anyone goes through a 30-year professional career without hitting the occasional roadblock. In my case, the biggest challenge I had to overcome was escaping from a trap of my own making. About 20 years into my career, I had become fixated on achieving the top job at the company. I made big sacrifices, said yes to jobs I didn't really want, and volunteered for unpopular projects.

'One day, things came crashing down around me. An unexpected big reorganization was announced, and when the music stopped, I wasn't offered the chair I thought I deserved. It was a big surprise and quite traumatic. I think I went through the stages of grief, denial, and anger.'

Trisha recalls how, while painful at the time, it forced an important re-evaluation. 'I think something about the whole situation made me look more closely at myself. Ironically, I realized that I had allowed myself to get wrapped up in playing the wrong game.'

Trisha's soul searching led to the realization that she needed and deserved more from her work. She soon resigned her executive position to join the management team for a small renewable energy company that had never previously included HR at the executive table. 'It was the biggest single gamble I've made in my career, from predictable big corporate, to dynamic entrepreneurial venture. It turned out to be the best professional decision I've ever made. I got to do work I really cared about, that led directly to something important, and I got to do it with a small group of leaders I really respected.'

My Career Tip

'Strive to keep balance in your professional life.' Trisha believes that it's when we get too narrowly focused that we can make mistakes. 'Particularly those of us who are very driven to achieve goals and results, we must be especially careful not to get carried away. It's surprisingly easy to persuade yourself that sacrificing fulfilment and meaning for a reward makes sense, when the reality is the reverse.'

Roman Schindler
Sportsperson, Entrepreneur, and Influencer

Roman's story talks to the difficulty of getting caught in a literal career game. His story also shows how overcoming adversity can help us become more resilient... help us learn important habits about self-reliance, discipline, and setting positive goals.

My early career was literally killing me... here's how I escaped

'From an early age I dreamed of being a professional football player. I believed it was my destiny.' At age seven Roman joined a Vienna Club, and at age 21 he was team leader of Bradley University Soccer Team, at the highest National Collegiate Athletic Association (NCAA) Division One College League.

'Elite sports are highly competitive; sacrifice, and a degree of suffering, comes with the territory,' says Roman. 'I had experience in fighting through adversity. As a child I was diagnosed with cancer. The experience made me mentally tough. The trouble to some extent though is getting trapped on a course where you accept more and more suffering, losing sight of what might be more important.'

Roman suffered a series of concussions, seven in fact, during his professional football-playing career. The doctors told him he risked serious long-term injury if he continued. 'As simple and straightforward as it may sound to hear doctors advising you that your career was killing you, it wasn't that simple for me. This was my destiny... my dream... or so I believed. I had tunnel vision.'

What happened to change Roman's mind? What made him step back and re-evaluate?

'Well, it was literally a blunt trauma to my head... as I walked slowly off the field after suffering my last concussion, I had a moment of realization. It was strange because it felt like time stood still a little. I wasn't aware of the crowd, the coaches, the other players. I seemed to have a moment of complete tranquillity. I remember very clearly an internal dialogue playing out as I walked. I knew it was time to choose a new path. What stunned me most was a sense of relief... excitement almost. I was not disconsolate or downbeat… more like a load had been lifted.'

What does life look like beyond football (soccer)?

'Ultimately, the other side of football, life is great! I'm so much happier now. I have discovered aspects of life, things that make me happy and fulfil me, that I never would have discovered had it not been for my big reinvention.'

Roman turned his lifelong passion for fitness and training into a different, more purposeful pursuit. He focused on shaping his mind, his body, and his personality. He subsequently won the high-profile Mr Austria contest. He now provides sports and psychology training, motivational talks, and is writing his first book. All at the age of 28!

'Honestly, the best piece of career advice I could give, is to be proactive in adapting and reinventing yourself. It's too easy to get fixed on just one thing. Being focused and super disciplined can be a critical skill for realizing your dreams… but it can also stop you from pausing to understand the consequences – serious, dangerous consequences – if you keep going in just one direction. It's sort of like banging your head against a wall.'

Chapter 8

Don't become a captive of the career game

This chapter deals with how we play games in our careers. Not as in team building or video games, but in a sense of seeing patterns and behaviours that we think will help us achieve our short-term goals, extrapolating these and leveraging them without deeper thought about collateral damage or longer-term consequences.

Let's start by persuading you that we all do this. To some degree or other, we all participate in game playing. When we interview for jobs, we rehearse what we think the interviewers will want to hear. When we submit our resumé, we look to follow and amplify clues we see in the job description. When we start a new job, we pay careful attention to how others behave, and we start to mimic them. We study our bosses closely, seeing them as our ultimate role model, and we play out a sort of Oedipus complex, where our boss is our father and their job/status is our mother.[1]

Does any of this ring true?

What about company systems and processes? When it comes to the annual performance review, how do you approach it? Do you try to figure out how to present your own contribution and value? In a calendar year's performance cycle, are you conscious of 'promoting' and 'marketing' your most important achievements? Indeed, do you time major project milestones for the end of the year to maximize recency bias?[2]

And at the pinnacle of this game playing, the Mount Everest of short-cutting systems for personal goals, the collateral damage and moral jeopardy increase exponentially. Initially, it can seem very innocent and harmless. However, game playing, at its essence, is looking to take some advantage from the system or tactics used to achieve a more collective goal or outcome. Game playing is entirely selfish as it focuses on the system apparatus, absolves us of how our actions impact the ultimate outcomes, and instead looks exclusively on maximizing our own reward. The moral self-justification that we associate with some of the great corporate scandals of the last 50 years have their foundations in similar distorted equivalences. Yes, our bank has failed and needs a public bailout, but we have earned those big bonuses. The product doesn't really work, but let's not tell these investors, we need to 'fake it until we make it'. Let's ignore the rules about using depositors' funds to shore up the trading business positions. I've a good feeling we can make all the losses back.

We are surrounded in our professional lives with reminders of how our work is a game. Our family and friends will remind us, 'Yeah, I know it doesn't make sense, but just give THEM what they want,' or simply, 'Hey, you need to PLAY THE GAME if you want to get on.' Throughout our lives we naturally look for ways to make sense and simplify every complex system we encounter.

From our early educations, from seeking patterns in academic subjects and school grading systems, all the way through to figuring out how to get a discount on the next big purchase we plan to make. We are wired to assume there is a shortcut, a hack, a secret backdoor.

The first big takeaway from *A Groundhog Career* is to demonstrate the dangers of game playing at work. When we reduce our careers to a game, when we operate with only one definition of success, and when we chase only the glitz and glamour of material success, we can become a prisoner of the game. A little like in the Disney movie *Tron*, although to stay with our groundhog metaphor we should pick instead from all the movies that seek to demonstrate how you can become trapped living the same day repeatedly, caricaturing the definition of madness... repeating the same actions expecting a different outcome.

Having persuaded you that we all participate in game playing, let us now set our sights on explaining (1) why this is entirely natural human behaviour, and (2) how we should set our sights not on complete abstinence but on being far more attuned and sensitive to how and when we use games, understanding the price we pay for doing so, and, in particular, being extremely cautious not to let them define us.

Why game playing is an entirely natural human behaviour

Game playing is an extension of our natural sensemaking processes. It's a very human, and even healthy, thing for us to do.

The scientific research into how human beings process complex problems tells us that the use of heuristics, of making connections and equivalencies, is foundational.[3] From our earliest incarnation as a species 100,000 years ago, the ability to distinguish threats from opportunities was core to our survival. The survival of the fittest instinct helped us develop powerful flight, fright, and fight instincts. In some ways, we would argue our very DNA equips us with a complex hard-coded thinking apparatus designed to ensure our survival. It processes enormous amounts of information from all our senses and makes instant assessments about their immediate threat.[4]

A great deal of research has been conducted into how our brains have evolved to make sense of our world. We would point first to the father of modern psychology Sigmund Freud.[5] He theorized that our consciousness was divided between the **id**, our impulsive base instincts, **superego**, the morally aware voice of reason, and the **ego** that referees an eternal conflict between the first two. In Freud's view, humans live in constant battle with themselves. Our base desires are personified by the id, compelling us constantly to fulfil our own selfish needs, and the more civilized and society-conditioned superego judging us for our squalid base inclinations.

Recently, Steve Peters has built a modern model from Freud's foundations naming our three conflicting thinking processes as: (1) the **chimp**: the impulsive urge to follow your instincts, (2) the **computer**: the part of our brain that is more analytical, understands social and moral matters, and tries to moderate our actions, and (3) the **human**: the conscious thinking part of our brain that seeks meaning and that decides whether the Chimp or Computer should win the day.[6]

So, let us put this in the context of work and game playing. In simple terms, we are compelled by our **id** or **chimp** to grab any opportunity to shortcut the system and jump the queue, to leapfrog ahead. Our **superegos** or **computers** try to intervene… scolding us for our nihilistic selfish thoughts. This creates a mental tug of war some of which we are conscious of, but according to all the research, most of the time we are blissfully unaware of the inner turmoil. We may grab the second piece of cake or eat the last cookie without any great conscious soul searching.

Where Freud and Peters help us understand what's going on in our brains, Daniel Kahneman goes a step further.[7] In *Thinking Fast and Slow*, he offers a simpler explanation for how we behave, explaining that we make a spontaneous prioritization of whether any tasks we face can be answered quickly by our intuitive sense or whether they require pondering and careful analysis. The key differentiator is our motivation when we encounter the problem. Are we focusing on our short-term needs, on getting a promotion or a bigger pay raise, or are we focused on something with a longer time frame and a deeper purpose? The thinking processes we employ and the resulting calculations we make will be profoundly different.

The world (and our brain) sometimes encourages us to focus on the wrong things

How we view our objective is the critical point. What are we primarily interested in achieving? Launching into a professional career is something most of us attempt in our late teens or early 20s. It can be a very stressful and intimidating challenge. We are simultaneously navigating a separation from our parents, guardians, and teachers as the primary authority figures in our lives, and assuming those responsibilities ourselves. In the process, we are still developing our sense of who we are, how the world works, what opportunities are available, and how to make the best of what we see.

The very natural and quite understandable default position we adopt is to follow a path of expectations. We are guided by parents, relatives, friends. We take advice from teachers and careers advisors. We look at what our friends are doing. We filter all of this through what we believe at the time is a hierarchy of desirability. When a big consulting firm, a Wall Street bank, or a tech company invite us to apply for an internship or graduate training programme, most of us make the assessment that this is a top echelon opportunity. Perhaps, we have a mental model that is something like this:

Tier 1a: Offer to join top graduate programme in banking, tech, or consulting.

Tier 1b: Successfully pitch for funding or join an existing start-up.

Tier 2: Offer to join graduate programme of any Fortune 100 company.

Tier 3: Offer from any recognizable company for a respectable position.

Tier 4: Any job offer… from anyone… of any kind.

Tier 5: Crap… crap… crap… what am I going to do…

Maybe your list was/is a little different, but the point is most of us started with a ranked list, based on perceived desirability, of what we saw as the available career options. That we do this is completely understandable and a sign of logical thinking! We have, after all, been working toward exactly this goal since age five or six when we started school. Much of our education system is focused on giving us knowledge and acclimatizing us toward that fatal day when we leave school and go to join the world of the (self-) employed.

We feel the weight of expectations from our family, which are typically assuaged by who we work for, how much money we make, and success is most easily expressed by promotions and the trappings of office. Our friends compete and we don't want to miss out. The fear-of-missing-out (FOMO) effect takes hold.[8] We become envious of those who get jobs in the city, drive expensive cars, live in expensive parts of the city, and holiday in fashionable resorts. The magazines we read, the shows we watch, the news we consume, the social media images of beautiful people, all subliminally suggest to us what we should be trying to achieve.

Over the years, psychologists have staged various experiments that help us understand the link between apparent irrational human behaviour and things like authority (Milgram's electric shocks), conformity (Asch's the short line is longer), and fairness (Brosnan and de Waal's capuchin monkeys).[9] You may not be surprised to learn that all these things shape how we define our initial career objectives. And our external points of reference tell us that we must be on the right path. Multiple studies have found a link between our brain releasing dopamine when we are given praise, a compliment, or win a competition. Dopamine is a neurotransmitter that stimulates the reward centre in our brains. Getting a job that impresses our parents equals a hit of dopamine. Beating others to a first promotion, another hit. And so on.

Shey Sinope and the groundhog career

In Shey's story, we caricature how this can play out by turning the chase for career progression into a game. We set the scene for why Shey finds it seductive, why he thinks it's what he wants, and how he measures his progress. It was intended to be an absurd and amusing twist, but have we exaggerated that much? Many companies use systems to help them manage their human resources. Performance ranking systems not so long ago were widespread and attempted to compare relative performance each year. Potential was measured using a nine-box grid. The idea was that people would be ranked based on upward potential and horizontal performance. Then there are self-assessment forms and 360-degree reviews. In the late 1980s and 1990s lots of companies, perhaps inspired by GE or some of the business literature of the era, believed internal talent systems could provide a flawlessly meritocratic platform to identify and nurture the best talent. It turns out that these systems weren't nearly as effective as initially believed. In many cases, rather than identify and promote the best talent, they simply created lots of mini-mes.

We enjoyed playing with some popular psychometric tests in Chapter 2 through the assessment centre that Shey visits as part of his final day for the CAPs programme. The chapter lent itself to following Shey as he was put through his paces. These open-ended games are wonderful things to poke fun at. We have occasionally found ourselves discussing these things with people who haven't been through them. The looks on their faces when they say, 'Now hang on a minute… they were told what again… to dismantle a nuclear device using a coat hanger and a three-year-old copy of the *New York Times*… that's bizarre… why don't people just say… no… no thank you! And walk away?' The answer is obvious. They believe that there is a pot of gold somewhere at the end of that particular mushroom cloud.

Shey's formula for success is our made-up construct. While it may be interesting to hear the outcome of anyone brave enough to try it in real life, we do not recommend it. Not necessarily because it wouldn't work in the short term to garner a measure of superficial success; we have reason to believe it might! The real danger of Shey's formula is it does not calculate the collateral damage. If you had people in an organization that paid no heed to how their actions impacted colleagues, customers, products, laws, reputations, relationships, or communities, then our prediction is that that organization would spectacularly implode fairly quickly.

The evil genius of Shey in the fable is that he takes advantage of those who attempt a more authentic approach. The suggestion is that if you are alone or in the small minority of people who focus only on your own selfish needs, you might be able to gain a short-term advantage. Ultimately, however, two things will catch up with you: (1) like all charades, at some stage the hoax is revealed, and (2) the protagonist eventually realizes they have become trapped in an endless game from which it's hard to escape.

Getting trapped in the game – dealing with the consequences

Daniel Kahneman observed that the way we frame our goals creates the context for our actions.[10] It creates a tunnel in our minds with the goal at the end, and we visualize the fastest route to our destination. When we define our career goals as advancement, pay raises, promotion, purely climbing the career ladder, we use all our human ingenuity to achieve those aims. In the process, we justify ourselves by telling ourselves that the 'ends justify the means'. We find reasons to reassure ourselves that we are not alone in striving for the same things. Like witnessing people cutting in line on the motorway, people tussling to buy the last toilet rolls during the pandemic, the crowds who scramble for the best sale deals on Black Friday, or attempting to grab the last must-have Christmas toy for our kid, we see the world as binary... it's us or them... win or lose... live or die. Our chimp brain or id takes control and creates an irresistible impulse in us to focus only on our own wants.

The big problem is we don't consider the consequences. We live very much in the moment. The universe collapses for us and there is no future, no past, just the now. Equally, we see the world in a crystal clear way, albeit through a cognitively distorted lens; there is what we want and everything else is an obstacle to be conquered.

But there are consequences to this behaviour, and to this self-justifying selfishness.

First, our behaviour creates an escalation of commitment. While we don't see it initially, we are inadvertently committing ourselves to a way of behaving. What happens if you set out to achieve something, cut corners, absolve yourself of any responsibility for collateral damage, stick your elbows out and charge... only to find you don't quite get the reward you wanted? What do you do next? Double-down? Go harder?

We are reminded of the extraordinary novel by Bret Easton Ellis, *American Psycho*.[11] Obviously, his central protagonist has some very twisted 'issues' beyond our intended purpose here but the reference punctuates our point. As you go down this path, it becomes increasingly difficult to stop escalating. It's like running on a treadmill with no stop button that just gets faster and faster, or finding yourself trapped in a 'gilded cage', a hostage to your own selfish actions with no obvious means of escape.

The second consequence is that if you look for validation and accomplishment purely from external sources, particularly superficial career ladder measures, you will find they have an extraordinarily limited shelf life. The first promotion may feel great, and you may enjoy basking in what you believe to be the adulation of family, friends, and colleagues. But the second won't have the same impact and the tenth will hardly move the needle at all. There is a huge body of research that tells us that this is true. From Abraham Maslow, through Frederick Herzberg, to Richard Easterlin and the paradox that carries his name, we know that human happiness and fulfilment is NOT correlated with accumulating more of the same.[12,13,14] Once we have ticked the box of financial security and proven ourselves comparably capable to others, we are compelled to look for other ways to test and improve ourselves.

The final consequence is possibly the most dangerous of all. We give ourselves reasons to paint ourselves as monsters. Only very few of us can completely insulate ourselves from the feeling that we are cheating, racking up a body count, and leaving mayhem in our wake. We don't just carry this burden; it accumulates over time to a point where it interferes with our ability to operate in a healthy way. We become haunted by our repressed sense of morality.

There is perhaps some dark irony in the observation that the very people you wanted to impress, your parents, your family, your friends, might discover that you are a fraud. That a growing voice inside you tells you that any acknowledgement and recognition you received was undeserved. We call this *building a personal authenticity deficit*, which we become increasingly aware of and that ultimately paralyzes us. As time goes by, what starts as fleeting, nagging doubts, grow to become a tsunami of negativity that interferes with our sleep, eats away at our self-confidence, and destroys our self-worth.

How do you avoid becoming a prisoner of the career game? Of waking up one day and finding yourself despairing the day ahead? This is one of the insidious aspects of the *career game trap*. It creeps up on you. Day by day, you dig yourself a little deeper. Little by little you construct the walls around you. Week by week you accumulate 'trappings' that are designed to remind you of your good fortune, but in reality, they are more like gilded bars that encircle your conscience.

At some point the walls start to feel like they are closing in. You feel like you are suffocating. You aren't sure how you got there but you know the day ahead will not be pleasant. That work is not fulfilling and carries no meaning, but you feel obligated. Obligated in part to continue the charade, to perpetuate the game, but also because you have created a lifestyle that is dependent on it. Bills, mortgages, not to speak of the obligations you have made to others. Work projects you have committed to deliver. Meetings you have scheduled. People who you tell yourself may be counting on you to suffer so they can be free.

How to avoid, or escaping the career game trap

Well, there is hope. In our work, we have helped thousands of people to navigate this space. We have distilled the thousands of career conversations, existential crises, and tens of thousands of hours of mentorship into what we believe are the three most powerful principles, and supported them with four suggested thinking/reflection exercises:

1. **Challenge whether you have become a prisoner to the career game**

    We don't wish to sound Pollyanna-ish about this first point, particularly because we know that finding ways to simplify and navigate work can often seem like game playing. We aren't saying you should completely abstain from looking for patterns, shortcuts, or mental hacks that help you better understand how organizations and careers work. What we are saying is don't make the mistake of confusing how you perform in a career game as the only thing that matters. At best, performing well in achieving corporate ladder milestones is a means to an end. They cannot be the end. They offer a fool's gold, a form of alchemy that can look like a quick way to turbo charge your career, but they flatter to deceive. Like the legendary mermaid stories from old sailors, they sing a beguiling song that will ultimately lure you onto treacherous rocks.

Thinking exercise #1: Can you answer three levels of why?

A trick we use to tease out whether someone has become captive of game playing is to see if they can explain what they are doing to three levels of why:

Why 1: The obvious first level – Often expressed in different forms of what you are trying to achieve through your job this year.

Why 2: The next level of why – Typically expressed as what you want to achieve after succeeding with level 1.

Why 3: Searching for the deepest motivation and explanation – The elusive 'why'... often the level rarely thought about... how does this help you get closer to something that can only be described in qualitative terms?

This exercise helps us stretch our thinking beyond the immediacy of what is happening today. It requires us to widen the context of what we may be narrowly focused on and forces us to consider how that fits within a wider and deeper context.

We can easily fall into the trap of believing that fighting for the next promotion is our only purpose. If you believe that achieving a short-term goal is the only thing that matters, we want to help you reframe your thinking to stretch your view toward some deeper more overarching purpose.

This exercise is a good thinking exercise to do every month to challenge yourself, but it is at its most powerful when you discuss it with a trusted thought partner – someone like Shey's Uncle Freddy, for example. Most of us have a mentor, respected role model, or a friend we trust to be constructively honest with us. Equally, if you have the opportunity as part of your work network to have a quarterly or bi-annual career discussion with someone who you trust to challenge your thinking, try doing this exercise with them. Give them permission to challenge your answers and dig to see how convincing you are when you share your answers. Leave time for them to play back their reflections and ask them whether they saw flaws or holes in your thinking.

2. **Challenge yourself to make sure that what you are doing today is the best way to get where you want to go**
   Do you have a career plan? Do you have a clear distinction about how the job you are doing today

will help you get where you'd like to be in five and ten years' time? The most important thing is framing your current job in the context of how it helps you move forward.

To perform well in our jobs, we must be present in the now and ensure we don't wish away the days until we can do something else. There is, however, a difference between simply dreaming about being somewhere else, somewhere better, daydreaming about being on some glorious beach, versus being motivated to achieve something in the short term that will likely give us the opportunity to do or experience or achieve something down the road.

The key here is to be able to understand your goals in terms of how they allow you to stretch from the base of Maslow's pyramid, beyond material and quantitative measures to more qualitative and personal discovery objectives.

Thinking exercise #2: Visualizing what an improved 'you' looks like

Take some time out, ideally in a place that allows you to detach from the hustle and bustle of everyday tasks. Sometimes this might be a long run around the park, a leisurely coffee at your favourite café, or the favourite spot where you go to find a pocket of tranquillity.

Take a note pad or open the notes section of your device (while making sure you quiet the notifications) and try to write down the answers to these questions:

Q1: Project yourself ten years into the future. How could you improve your belief, increase your confidence by at least 10%, that you were spending the majority of your time doing something you cared passionately about? Something that you believed mattered and, crucially, made a positive difference to people you care about. What might that look like? Who and why did you choose what you chose?

Q2: In what way does your work, your career, play a role in achieving the above? How does work enable you to progress toward what you pictured in the first question? Is it the direct vehicle of achieving it (i.e. a business mechanism to tackle the climate emergency) or indirect (i.e. something that enables you to achieve something else)?

Q3: How far away from your answer to the second question are you today? Are you on the right road or not even in the same postcode? Try to describe the gap you see between where you are today and where you pictured you'd like to be.

Q4: What is one positive step you could make in the next month that would close the gap? Think about this in terms of getting 1% better every day. Even a determination that you want to get out of the corporate rat race and start your own business starts with the first small step of writing down a business pitch deck you can start to circulate for potential backers. Moreover, the idea that tomorrow you could be 1% closer to your imagined future is entirely practical.

3. **Write down your red lines and find a mechanism to hold yourself to account**

The trouble with matters of moral and ethical integrity is that we forget they require constant attention. We often think of these as sporadic challenges that declare themselves to us at specific points in our careers. 'Sir, we have come to the time in the meeting where we must now challenge your personal integrity... please select the blue pill or the red pill.' This is not how it happens. By the time our imagined pinstripe suit wearing, bespectacled general counsel has handed us the pills, we have likely already compromised ourselves.

We stress this point constantly when we talk with people struggling with career decisions. Moral jeopardy is a constant challenge. Our integrity is under attack every day. From witnessing poor behaviour in the office and not calling it out to the seemingly innocuous action of condoning our own cutting in line at the underground station.

Falling into the career game trap is to some extent a failure of our own capacity to control our base impulses. We suspend our moral compass for a few years until we have the luxury of having established ourselves. It's easy to tell ourselves that we will return to our ethical principles once we've got the next promotion, received the big bonus, or won whatever competition we've set for ourselves. The trouble is our misdeeds haunt us. Their shadow makes us more likely to continue to compromise and make excuses.

Thinking exercise #3: Maintaining your cabal of trusted advisors

Create and leverage a personal cabal of people you can be completely honest with about what you are doing in your career. People you trust to be objective, to be sufficiently distant from the specifics to be able to point out any errors in your thinking but informed enough to know the business realities. Give them permission to call you out. No spin, no gloss, just brutal honesty.

Name your cabal: We all need a list of nine to 15 people in our lives that form an inner trusted circle. We call this your cabal. The people in your life that you can count on to support you, to advise you, and to give you the jolts you need.

Write them down: This is an important list. Sometimes we find people struggle to find nine. Challenge yourself to think of the Uncle Freddy's in your life. Most of us have two or three. Then if you still haven't gotten to at least nine, think about people from school, from work, friends, business acquaintances, and ask yourself, 'Are these people I really respect, from whose opinions and perspective I might really benefit?' If the answer is yes, ask them if they would mind occasionally letting you bounce work-related challenges off them. In our experience 99% of them will say… sure.

Find a reason to check in with one of them every month: When there is something pressing, it's always instinctive to pick up the phone, text, or email for advice. But the real trick here is to seek counsel even when you don't think there is anything urgent. It's the quiet moments that are often the most important to refresh and renew our resolve. What matters to us? How far are we prepared to go to get it? Along the way, what will we never compromise?

4. **Measure your 'giving and taking' balance of payments**

A 2007 study in *Nature Neuroscience* found that only between 1% and 2% of the world population are true empaths.[15] And just a further 20% display some empathetic qualities. By this measure, eight out of ten people really struggle to empathize. There are again very rational explanations for why we are oblivious or even sincerely uncaring of how our behaviour impacts those around us. The selfish gene is strong in most of us.

To test whether we are conscious of the emotional fallout zone we may create around us, we find it can be quite sobering to ask people to take an occasional inventory. The exercise helps us come to terms with two things: (1) how much carnage we can leave in our wake, and (2) challenge ourselves to ask was it all necessary?

Thinking exercise #4: Testing that you can explain your work on at least three levels

On a Friday evening or Saturday morning, take the time to reflect on your week. Pull up your work calendar and review the meetings and interactions you had during the week.

Step 1: Create a grid on a piece of paper: make two columns. In the first column, write POSITIVE and in the second write NEGATIVE.

Step 2: For each meeting, force yourself to think about how your behaviour left the people you met with. Did they leave the meeting, on balance, positive and motivated about themselves or negative and disillusioned? Put a check against just one column for each meeting. If there was more than one person in the meeting, rate the overall tone you think the audience left with.

Step 3: In grading each meeting, be careful to challenge yourself. Separate out your impact from whatever else took place. Were you aggressive, competitive, did you call people out, did you try to repackage an idea as your own, did you interrupt, were you dismissive, did you fire any zingers?

Step 4: Total the columns and subtract the negatives from the positives.

Business is not always 'fun' but there is a line between seeking great outcomes and doing so while affording those around us the dignity, respect, and politeness we know costs very little. If you have a negative total for your week, ask yourself, 'Was that really necessary? Could I have handled that differently?' Indeed, think about whether your desire to win or simply be proven right came at a greater cost. Did you derail the meeting, shut down a voice or opinion, win the battle but lose the war?

If you have a big negative, consider two things: (1) On Monday, seek out those you may have had the most negative impact on and apologize. See if you can repair the damage. And (2) Challenge yourself to get a better score next weekend.

Chapter blink

- Using heuristics to help us understand and explain the complex systems around us is a natural human evolutionary trait.

- Heuristics, hacks, and rules of thumbs are translated into games that we are inducted into when we enter the workplace.

- Our instincts to compete and focus on winning can lead us to become myopically focused and narrow our thinking in an unhealthy way.

- When we start our careers, we fight to establish ourselves; in the process we are more susceptible to exaggerate and overcompensate for our insecurity.

- When we focus on only the superficial aspects of our career, we end up getting trapped by a dangerous escalation of self-destructive behaviours.

- Focus on qualitative not purely quantitative measures of success.

- Balance your short- and long-term career objectives. Know the difference between repeating versus progressing each day.

In three phrases

1. WANTS VERSUS NEEDS – be careful what you wish for. You might get it.

2. QUALITY NOT QUANTITY – have an answer to why you do what you do.

3. LOOK TO THE HORIZON – there are hidden costs to be paid for only maximizing the now.

Daniel Obst
President and CEO of AFS Intercultural Programs

Daniel's story illustrates choices about things that matter in life, and the ability to find your purpose. It's the story of a leader who went out to explore the Big Apple in pursuit of dotcom riches. Instead, he found himself, what matters to him, and his purpose in life. Helping next generation leaders to find and purpose their professional passions.

Here is how I found my purpose

Ever since I was about 11 years old, I wanted to be a 'diplomat' – although I wasn't entirely sure what that would entail. Or perhaps a flight attendant. Either way, I clearly wanted to experience the world beyond me.

I grew up in Berlin, Germany, the son of an American father and a German mother, and with adopted siblings from Cambodia, India, and Colombia. So perhaps it was growing up in a cross-cultural environment, where our parents taught us about the value of diversity and empathy.

As I reflect on my career journey now, I can see clearly that at some point my childhood dreams and sense of purpose were overtaken by commercial pragmatism or 'real-world' considerations.

After attending university in the United States and graduate school in England, I was offered an extraordinary opportunity with a brand-new tech start-up in New York City. It was 1998 and the height of the dotcom bubble. It was an intoxicating time and I think I was carried along by the collective euphoria and possibly 'irrational exuberance' of the time.

It was exciting... until the bubble burst!

Afterward, I had some time to re-evaluate. It felt to me like a spell had been broken. Purely chasing riches in the tech space just didn't feel quite right for me.

This is when I think I reconnected with my idealistic youth. I was offered an opportunity with the Institute of International Education: and from day one there I knew I had found my purpose. For 15 years at IIE, I had the most incredible opportunities to contribute to amazing public diplomacy projects in places such as Iran, Iraq, Cuba, Libya, Myanmar – countries where diplomatic relations were strained or non-existent. As challenging as these projects were, I had never previously felt so deeply invested in working to make things better.

Now I lead AFS Intercultural Programs, a 100-year-old global NGO focused on developing active global citizens through intercultural exchanges and youth empowerment programmes such as the AFS Youth Assembly.

I love what I do now – and I wouldn't change a thing about my career journey. My early work experience at the tech start-up helped me understand what it means to be entrepreneurial and innovative – something that comes in handy at a century-old organization!

Perhaps I didn't quite become a diplomat, but I have a suspicion my 11-year-old self would approve. The substance of what I do today is very much in keeping with my idealized childhood dream of working for a better future.

The best advice I can give to anyone is really understand your values, what matters to you, and what impact you want to make in the world – and then go for it.

Rohan Radhakrishnan
Co-Founder at Quarter Proof

Rohan's career follows the classic advertising and creative agency path... then takes an unexpected left turn. He took the familiar steps from university, internships, and then first job. 'I don't know how I chose the path, it found me. I had a talent for sales and creative design and the market told me I was in demand.

'I think of my career to this point as having had three distinct phases. In the first phase I was in awe of the business world, in love with what I was doing. The second, was getting caught up in the superficiality of upgrading jobs. It was just too seductive. The trouble is eventually you realize there are hidden agendas, and that world can be rather callous. The third phase, well, that was when I realized that the only person stopping me from doing something cool, with people I respected, was me.'

Rohan is now one of the UK's leading low alcohol beverage entrepreneurs. He and his co-founder have taken Quarter Proof to the leading edge of the drinks industry, famously turning down a *Dragon's Den* offer, to build a brand everyone under 40 is now talking about.

Looking behind the façade

When asked about the most defining moments in his career to date, Rohan recalls how he painfully came to realize that the professional world can be very cynical, transactional, and one dimensional. 'I think I saw what I wanted to see and then I realized I was really deluding myself. I believed in the broader story of what our business was doing… and, yes… I also thought I was pretty good at my part. However, after a tough year working to achieve some unrealistic goals, it became clear the leadership didn't really care about me. They saw me as an instrument, a means to an end.

'After a particularly traumatic series of sales pitches, I had a conversation with my bosses. Rather than encouragement and constructive brainstorming… I saw a glimpse of something darker and manipulative. It was simultaneously shocking and sobering. It was like a thin veneer was ripped off the world… I could finally see what was going on underneath the façade. All the other things I'd dismissed as just my imagination suddenly made sense.'

Rohan knew in that instant he was somewhere he never intended to be and on a trajectory he never consciously chose. He resigned. In the days that followed, he rebuilt a career path for himself. 'I started with what I wanted to do. That started with what I knew I was good at.' He quickly tested his ideas and found three charter clients willing to bet on him.

'It was incredibly liberating and life-affirming. Once I realized people saw value in what and how I wanted to go about things… well, it just seemed to create a virtuous circle for me.' He credits this moment as what set him on his course for his Quarter Proof destiny.

Career tips

'Well, I think based on my experience the two big lessons would be: (1) Be careful not to get seduced by the superficial aspects of professional life. People will often tell you what they think you want to hear… especially if it means they get something they want out of you in exchange, and (2) Should you come across things that seems too good to be true, it probably means you are paying a hidden price… one that perhaps you really can't afford in the long run.'

Chapter 9

Pursue your career not someone else's

Are you in a profession of your choosing, your design, or is it what other people expect you to do? Perhaps it's just an accident, a series of unexamined choices you hardly remember making that have led you down a path to where you are today. Does the work you do actually matter to you? Or is it simply something you do to earn a salary and pay the bills? Have you created a life for yourself where you must work to pay the bills, and you have persuaded yourself that you can't live without the things that create the bills?

Do you know why you are doing what you're doing? Do you know what it's all for? Are you confident that there is a compelling reason, a goal, a destination you are aiming to reach, something worth fighting for?

A few people are certain about their purpose. They are born with an envious clarity that they have a mission. They possess a self-assuredness and unshakeable self-confidence to doggedly pursue that purpose. Perhaps Confucius, Plato, Aristotle, Alexander the Great, Genghis Khan, Marcus Aurelius, Leonardo da Vinci, Isaac Newton, George Washington, Mahatma Gandhi,

Winston Churchill, Nelson Mandela, Jeff Bezos, and Elon Musk are examples. Equally, perhaps, their legends have now erased any doubts or stumbles they experienced on their way to having their names indelibly written into history. Regardless, this chapter and this book isn't for these people.

It's for the rest of us. The vast, vast, majority of us. Those of us who are directly or indirectly looking to find or improve the answers to these questions: 'Why?' and 'What's this ultimately all for?'

Pew Research reports that as many as three-quarters of us, particularly in our early careers, aren't certain what our professional lives should look like.[1] In fact, the only thing we seem certain of is that our current job is probably not part of the answer. We wrote earlier about the startlingly high levels of dissatisfaction with work and of what we glean from the 'great resignation' of 2021 and 2022. In this chapter, we plan to dig deeper into understanding why we may feel unfulfilled, rudderless, or trapped in a work existence that we aren't certain is right for us.

Puppets on a grand stage

You are probably familiar with *The Matrix* movies but are you familiar with the origins of the concept?[2] The idea that we live in some form of elaborate simulation is a concept we can trace back to Plato.[3] However, perhaps encouraged by the film's popularity, modern philosophers and physicists have been busy debating how deep this rabbit hole may go.[4]

To our minds, this rather indulgent discussion probably provides more ammunition to those who point to the lack of utility and pragmatism among parts of the academic world, than it helps us answer anything particularly useful. This said, there is a thread here that helps us segue into the science behind explaining how we can easily get carried along by external forces. There is lots of evidence that most of us from our earliest childhood internalize and make our choices based on pleasing others, conforming to what we believe is expected of us, and emulating major role models in our lives. We are conditioned by the environment, our family, the socio-economic conditions, heritage, cultural tradition, and geography into which we are born. In some ways, we can see how that might be represented as living in a software program. Where we differ is that the program is (probably) not the product of a malevolent AI (although wait for another 50 years and that may change) but more one of human evolutionary conditioning.

The celebrated sociologist Erving Goffman, in his book, *The Presentation of Self in Everyday Life*, suggested that we could think of our behaviour as a performance in front of, and for, an audience.[5] He talked about how we are handed a proverbial script by observing how those around us act and behave. We take the cues from being praised, scolded, rewarded, and punished. As importantly, we see how our siblings, friends, and role models are treated by those around them and mimic what we believe will endear us.

Taking this a step further, Donald Winnicott's research demonstrated how this observation and conditioning in our childhood can reinforce how we need to work hard to be a 'good child' and not a 'bad child'.[6] Winnicott helps us understand why we 'put on a face' for the world that we are conditioned to believe is respectable and desirable. Of course, the corollary of this is the repression and fear that our true instincts, behaviours, and feelings may be unacceptable or deformed.

Choosing a professional mask

So, as we near the end of our schooling and look toward a first step in the professional world, we can't help but look externally for both what others think is desirable and what we think will please those closest to us. Virginia Satir, the great family therapist, coined the phrase 'people pleaser' to describe our need to obtain approval.[7] While we tend to use her phrase rather broadly nowadays, she was attempting to help us decode how the emotional 'matrix' around us tempts us to look outside of ourselves toward external sources of value, validation, self-worth, and identity.

Bringing this all together, we make the case that it is entirely natural, human, psychologically 'normal', to start our early careers not by reference to some deep conviction about what fulfils us, some kernel of belief that we have been put on this planet to achieve something specific, but instead to look at taking the easier path to conform and fit in. We measure this by what we think other people think is desirable. As we attempt our initial launch into professional life, start our first job, get our first promotion, the external validation that comes with this outwardly focused search for meaning starts to evaporate. In a nutshell, the mask we have chosen to wear starts to chafe. We start to look beyond the narrow confines of family and friends for validation and are dissatisfied with measuring our jobs through just one narrow lens.

This is where we return to Maslow's work and those who followed him. When we start our careers, we typically focus on satisfying the bottom of his pyramid – the primordial needs. Equally, we are conditioned to focus on external forms of validation and definitions of success. These don't last very long. Once we have checked these boxes they add little additional utility to us. To some extent, they start to become counter-productive. Our best analogy is like eating cake… the first slice is great… the fifth isn't really that enjoyable… and the tenth… well, that is torture.

Shey's story and struggle to find an identity of his own

In *A Groundhog Career*, we juxtaposition Shey as superficially successful but simultaneously lost. He has consciously chosen to 'win' at work. He has done this mainly because he felt a deep insecurity about his ability to achieve any type of desirable success. He looked out at the world and was intimidated by it. So, when he stumbles over a way to make progress, to obtain accolades, he grabs it. However, he is also running away from something. He is worried that he may be an empty vessel. That he has a vacuum or deficiency at his core. Rather than explore questions of who he may be, he avoids the subject. In his early exchanges with Ellen, he's really trying to prove something to himself. That the trappings of his job give him meaning, respectability, sustenance.

Searching for ways to feel superior is a means to camouflage self-doubt and sweep your own insecurities under the carpet. Ultimately, it's a form of escapism. Escapism and avoidance of the deeper more troubling question: 'What if this is all I am?' We underline how difficult this can be by showing Shey attempting an introspection exercise but finding ways to use it only to justify himself. He is protecting himself, choosing to swim in a small pond, for two reasons. First, he has found a 'game' that he thinks he can 'win'. Second, and this is the key point for this chapter, he has narrowed his world view to avoid any clutter, emotional entanglements, or messiness that might emerge from a more multi-faceted exploration of life, the universe, and everything.

The problem is that it becomes repetitive, unfulfilling, and ultimately self-destructive. The runway is short. For most of us, overcoming the anxiety of securing a job and then proving to ourselves that we are at least 'satisfactory' performers in the eyes of the world, takes about two to ten years. Beyond that, if that is the only dimension of life that you focus on, well, you really are in danger of repeating the same day for the rest of your life.

The danger is... at some point something breaks

We've talked about chasing only material rewards in your career and how this ultimately runs out of utility.

There are significant diminishing returns. But should you choose to believe that the material and superficial aspects of career ladders are your very identity, your very purpose, well, you will face significant disappointment. If you tell yourself that life is about becoming a Vice President, Managing Director, or CEO... and you then achieve it, well, what then?

When we narrow our goals solely to these materialistic pursuits, we build ourselves a virtual hamster wheel. A hamster wheel in a cosseted prison cell. This is a path that can only lead to two things: (1) A self-fulfilling prophecy that requires us to keep feeding our shallow egos, and (2) We run further and further away from our authentic selves. We become narcissistic monsters... a version of the Patrick Bateman character in Ellis' novel.[8] As we accumulate titles and status, we must eventually seek more... more... and more. We become obsessed, fixated, leading us to construct a prison of inauthenticity.

In psychology, we call this cognitive dissonance and evasion. You will have heard and perhaps experienced forms of 'imposter syndrome'. The feeling that you are not worthy of the recognition you receive. That you are unqualified to do your job or speak on a specific subject. These concepts emerge from the research of Leon Festinger and James Carlsmith.[9] In simple terms, the further we navigate away from our true, authentic selves, the greater the dissonance. If we allow it to go unchecked, like an elastic band, eventually something breaks.

All our research underpins how, when left untended for too long, almost everyone eventually runs out of runway. It becomes just impossible to run any faster. The personal prison walls start closing in. In short, we end up self-destructing in either small (most of us have minor confidence and identity crises at some point between our late 20s and mid-40s) or in incredibly spectacular and damaging ways.

The examples of very high-profile career implosions are not difficult to find: Andrew Neumann of WeWork, Elizabeth Holmes at Theranos, Steve Easterbrook at McDonalds, and of course, the US politician George Santos. Further back there was Denis Kozlowski of Tyco, Bernie Madoff, Sam Bankman-Fried; we might also include all the CEOs of the banks during the financial crisis.[10] However, our favourite is probably the colourful fraudulent socialite Anna Sorokin whose story and skills at deception still intrigue us today... did she know she was lying or had she invented a reality for herself where she thought it was all true? [11]

It's easy to dismiss these as the unrelatable pantomime villains that are portrayed in the media, but the reality is these were all human beings who found themselves caught in career traps of their own devilish construction. Their downfalls were spectacular burn-outs but the path that led them there were simple incremental steps, one foot in front of the other. As fascinating and intriguing as it is to pick apart what went wrong for these (in)famous *cause célèbre*, we are more concerned with the practical realities we all face as we navigate our careers.

The facts are, as we have shown in this chapter, we are propelled into professional life with generally external points of reference for success, validation, and desirability. We navigate the difficult transition from school to work, grabbing a firm hold on the first rung on a ladder. We need to prove to ourselves that we can master the rudimentary aspects of a job, to establish ourselves in the scary and unknown world of work. As we do, there is a real danger we get fixated, narrow our focus, and forget that there may be more to life. In the process, we blindly start climbing... sometimes for decades... before realizing that we don't know why we're doing it and it's now an awful long way down... and that becomes a powerful reason to avoid searching for better answers.

Choosing the red pill – making the career TR3C[12]

There is an alternative. A different path. Like the one from the famous poem framed as *hidden from view*.[13] Where instead of framing your career goals as silly games or solely seeking external sources of validation, you choose to dig deeper, think more broadly, explore facets of professional life that will ultimately prove far more sustainable and fulfilling. So, if you suspect you are living in a professional simulation, that your career choices are not your own but those of either a malevolent AI or you simply have a suspicion you may have been swept along by societal programming, what do you do?

Well, you take the red pill of course.

Escaping the career game, jumping off the relentlessly accelerating treadmill of pursuing purely superficial job-related rewards, is a lifelong journey. It's a journey that we might describe as a relentless search marked by challenges and obstacles, but which ultimately leaves you with a feeling of deep satisfaction. The best careers are really measured not by money, status, or material things, but by overcoming adversity, of fighting for a cause that transcends selfish motivations, along with building relationships with people who share your goals. In this sense, we might describe the journey as a self-aware, purposeful trek or **TR3C**. A journey across the mountain ranges of your individual and unique sources of joy, through the swamps of professional challenges and compromises, while taking the time to appreciate the warmth of those you feel kinship with.

A professional **TR3C** requires:

1. **The Will**: All journeys start with a first step.
2. **Reinvention**: Embrace and develop your ability to adapt and grow.
3. **3-Dimensional Perspective**: Challenging yourself to reframe how you hold the role work should play in your life.
4. **Cause**: The discovery of a compelling qualitative cause.

Live professional life on your own terms

You will have heard the overused quote attributed to Oscar Wilde: 'Be yourself... everyone else is already taken.' Whether Wilde uttered these words or not they still carry weight.[14] They capture an important essence of one of life's challenges. Like Socrates: 'To know thyself is the beginning of wisdom.'[15] These are now perhaps dismissed as clichés or platitudes. But there is a reason why they are widely circulated as memes and social media posts. They distil something important, eternal, elusive, and complex. The frustration with these quotes is that they poetically point out the *what* without any insights on the *how*.

The trouble is, the *how* is not only elusive, but it can also be tremendously painful:

1. **The Will**

   There are three ways we find the will to break free of being a prisoner of what we have dubbed the career game:

   a) **Crisis**: By far the most common occurrence is in response to some professional breakdown. Breakdowns come in many shapes and forms. However, what we point to here is an incident like the one caricatured in Shey's story. Something breaks. The classic incidents are the results of cumulative, self-destructive behaviours that result in an individual being forced to re-evaluate the road they are on.

   Examples of this might be failing to get a promotion you really wanted, conversely actually getting a promotion you wanted but paying a heavy price for it, or being exposed in some way. However, they take a wide form of Freudian self-destructive tics including poor behaviours, excessiveness, exaggerations, inappropriate humour, and unconsciously looking for ways to get ourselves in trouble. When we navigate a long way away from the ideal image of who we believe we are at our core, it results in these cries for help in the form of 'acting out'.

b) **Intervention**: The threat of being estranged from loved ones can also force us to re-evaluate the path we are on. The classic example here is of a partner forcing us to make a choice between personal relationship and professional goals. However, we have seen instances of parents, siblings, and trusted professional advisors creating the circumstances necessary to stop someone in their tracks and force them to re-evaluate.

c) **Cold turkey**: Finally, there is the 'I need to go find myself' category. It takes an enormous amount of self-awareness, self-discipline, and no small measure of courage to walk away from a successful career path in a belief that it may not ultimately be healthy or that it may be stopping you from finding something more important.

Going cold turkey used to be quite rare; however, over the past ten years we have seen an increasing number of people re-evaluating the role work should play in their lives. Gen Z, in particular, seem much more self-aware of the potential price they pay for giving in to unconstrainted job sacrifices.

Of course, the big question that follows is... how do you avoid running out of runway and find a healthier, more sustainable, trajectory?

We mentioned earlier, our goal was to try to understand, distil, and share the secrets of those individuals
who have found fulfilment and sustaining professional
satisfaction. Our research into the behavioural distinctions that separate those who report being engaged
in their work is that they have very distinctive ways of
relating to, and framing, the role work plays in their lives.

These distinctive attributes are the inspiration for
the remaining three-quarters of our **TR3C** mnemonic.
Together, they represent a very distinctive mental
outlook on professional life. If we boil these down, we
might be tempted to say that they represent an almost
binary choice between a view of professional life as a
game to be played to win versus a vehicle to realize some
deeper cause, or some means to deepen the quality of our
existence.

1. **Reinvention**

   Constructive   restlessness…   unbridled   curi-
   osity… intrepid exploration…

   One very effective way *not* to get trapped in
   a career game is to hold any specific job as transitory. If we are restless to learn new things, to
   understand what is beyond the horizon, then
   we are far less likely to get trapped by aspects of
   our current routine. Reinvention is easier in our
   early careers because we are striving to establish
   ourselves in a world when we feel slightly intimidated by those who have mastered their professional discipline. We can channel that insecurity
   in one of two ways: (1) We can paint those we
   work with as competitors and find ways to beat

them in the promotion and bonus game, or (2) We can look at how the jobs are changing and be first adopters in mastering the next wave of tools, concepts, and ideas.

However, it can be seductive, particularly as we get older, to become increasingly complacent… lazy even… to rest on our laurels… to bask in a false security that we have earned ourselves the privilege to relax, putting aspects of our jobs on autopilot. Of course, this is a fallacy. The world is constantly changing; we can either embrace the opportunity that comes with that change or become a victim of it.

Moreover, those individuals who retain and foster their enthusiasm to learn new things, to think critically about what and why they are in a particular job or profession, who engage in debate about how their industries and jobs will likely be impacted by the mega trends around them and find a sense of satisfaction gathering more knowledge… they report much higher levels of professional contentment. It's a self-fulfilling, self-propelling cycle. It's something that makes complete sense given what we know about the stages of human development and search for self-actualization.

2. **3-Dimensional perspective**
When we allow ourselves to be defined solely by external forces we fall foul of the *identity confusion paradox*. It's like operating in just one dimension. Put another way, it's the other side of the 'being

single-minded' coin. Sometimes it's necessary to concentrate on one task. Think about being a brain surgeon, for example. We would expect them to be completely focused on the operation at hand. But this is not a great formula for living your entire career.

An attribute of those who have achieved greater career fulfilment is depth. We describe this as holding a 3-dimensional perspective; in pursuing a professional life as the metaphoric stool supported by three legs. It is extraordinary how something apparently negative can become something positive when we reframe its context. When we are successful in this, we can draw energy from what we are doing. We feel more optimistic, strong, vital, resilient... and we build a virtual circle for ourselves, where we are propelled forward. Conversely, when we get this wrong and out of balance, energy is wasted... we feel tired... a negative cycle takes a grip... and we are pulled down.

Downward direction	versus	Upward direction
Now is all that matters		I know where I am heading
I hate my work		I love aspects of what I do
I'm surrounded by idiots		I know people who make me better

The first dimension is about timeframe. Operating only in the short-term paints you into a corner. It is better to have a view of what today's tasks enable three, five, ten years from now. This is the classic visualization of moving toward something desirable. Ideally, the destination should be something qualitative not quantitative. For example, by completing this difficult hospital residency, I will ultimately be able to open that family practice in my hometown. Or, by going through these rounds of capital raising, my business will finally get to fix something important for me/my family/my friends/the world!

The second dimension is massively overlooked but is so critical. We have worked with thousands of people over the years, many of whom seem convinced that their jobs suck in every dimension. When we change the conversation to identifying something they love to do at work, just one aspect of work that they are good at... every one of them eventually can find one thing. From as simple as mastering an aspect of Excel to model a problem to nailing a presentation to senior management. The point is that if we focus on what we hate it becomes an all-consuming, self-fulfilling prophecy. If, however, we focus on the things we think we are good at, that gives us a sense of accomplishment, pride even. A great starting point in any conversation about searching for meaning, fulfilment, and happiness in professional life, is to start by making an inventory of things you enjoy doing. If you make those the foundation of your career plan… you may be amazed by the results.

3. **Cause**

This is framing the individual aspects of a job, of our work, as a means to an end, and not the end itself.

The most powerful force in any professional journey is the belief that you are a warrior fighting for something transcendental. Cause in this sense cannot be something material. It is some outcome, some challenge, some problem that is greater than any one individual. The evidence for this statement is widespread. Great entrepreneurs, inventors, social activists, cultural icons, wouldn't have thought of their mission as the meetings, speeches, or presentations they did on any given day, but of how they might lead to something more inspiring such as curing a disease, ending suffering, raising the voices of the oppressed, or elevating art to a new standard.

The way we measure or describe a cause is very important. It helps us transcend the daily tyranny of short-termism and incrementalism. A cause in this sense can only be described in terms of a collective outcome. However, it is important to underline that it needn't be grandiose and world changing. The most important ingredient of a powerful cause is its meaning to you. Consider these examples:

- Ivan Roitt – a British oncologist.
- Jean Miller – a cloakroom attendant at Vidal Sassoon hair stylists.
- Tom Swan – runs a sweet shop in Scotland.
- Sidney Htut – a psychiatrist with the NHS.

All of these people have found a cause that has propelled them to enjoy incredibly fulfilling careers. How do we know? Their average age is 82... and they are still all working... healthy... energetic... enthusiastic... happy.[16] Neuroscientists have consistently pointed to the existence of a core purpose, a cause, as an essential ingredient in helping human beings retain vitality long into their twilight years. Sadly, the reverse is also true... the absence of a purpose seems to accelerate our mental and physical decline.[17]

Perhaps it's easy to guess Ivan's cause and perhaps Sidney's. They both work in healthcare, and in different ways, we can imagine their desire to help other people. However, what do you imagine Jean's cause might be? Or for that matter Tom? In their cases, it's less obvious. What they say is that they enjoy the social component of their work, both serving others but feeling part of a team, a community. As fascinating as each of these examples may be, our reason for sharing this list is to amplify that powerful causes can be found almost anywhere, in any profession, at any age.

The most common causes in our experience tend to fall into the following broad categories:

- Change – fighting for change… righting a wrong… improving the world.
- Love/Service – providing for or serving others.
- Problem solving – finding solutions to consequential problems.
- Creation/Invention – pursuit of artistic expression, beauty.
- Fellowship/Duty – *espirit de corps* and a sense of being needed.
- Adventure – seeing how far you can go literarily or metaphorically.

One final point on the subject of finding your compelling cause… they do tend to have a shelf life. In this sense they are a little like goals or perhaps more accurately, phases of our natural human life stages. The things we fight for in our adolescence tend to morph into different things in our 20s/30s, again in our mid-life, and at least one more time in our old age. Our context changes, we develop different perspectives and different priorities. We, generally, have access to more resources and, as we progress, we see new possibilities and opportunities. It is essential to be able to manage these transitions. This is where our **TR3C** mnemonic is designed to help reinforce how we need to think consciously and critically about 'why we are really doing this' and 'what's it all for?'

Reflection exercises

We will close this chapter with three thinking exercises designed to heighten your personal awareness of where you may be in your own career journey, while offering some suggestion of actions you might consider taking to help you 'escape' if you feel in danger of being trapped.

Thinking exercise #1: Following the white rabbit

Part A

Think about who you are when you are at work. Think about how you behave, what you say, how you say it, and how you process information and make decisions. Mark a Y on the spectrum below to signify where you think this is. It doesn't matter where you mark it so long as you're clear how you are measuring the left–right axis.

Now, think about who the 'real' you is... when you are at your best, the person you think you are at your core. Using the same criteria as you did for the Y... mark the real you as an X.

Part B

What's the most important thing in your career? Your overarching goal… the thing you are most concerned with achieving. Circle the letter below that most closely represents the timeframe in which you think you should be able to achieve that goal.

(a) Less than 12 months
(b) Between 1 and 3 years
(c) 3–10 years
(d) 10 years plus

Part C

Reflect on your answers to Parts A and B. If there is a distance between your X and Y in Part A, why is that? If your answer to Part B was three years or less, what does that mean?

Thinking exercise #2: Conscious inventory of where joy comes from

Take a moment to disconnect. If you are reading this book on a long-haul flight somewhere, that's perfect. Try to find some space and distance from your daily routine. Some people go for a long run, others practise yoga. Switch off your phone, close your laptop.

Part A

Take 20 deep breaths in and out. Count each one.

Part B

Think about a task, skill, or other achievement you personally completed in the last year that gave you a sense of satisfaction. Something you think you did really well. It doesn't matter how apparently trivial it was. If it gave you a sense of accomplishment, if it made you feel good, gave you a sense of pride, that's what's important.

Part C

Now, extrapolate whatever you visualized in B. If you had to categorize it, to describe it to a friend, a parent, a relative, a career coach or mentor, what was it about the task that caused you to feel joy?

Part D

Building on C, how could you plot a course in the next 12 months that would allow you to experience that feeling more frequently?

Thinking exercise #3: Take the TR3C challenge

Our goal in this chapter was to discuss three things: (1) Why it's quite natural for us to wonder if we are on a path of our own choosing; (2) The traits that seem to define the highest levels of satisfaction and fulfilment in career journeys; and (3) How we can all set a course to achieving higher levels of satisfaction, fulfilment, and sustainable professional success. Our final thinking exercise builds on this last part and suggests how you can take some concrete steps if you feel the need.

We think it's a good idea to take your reflections from reading this chapter and turn them into a rough career plan. The process helps you work through what you really want, what you really enjoy, and how you plot a course to do more of that. Career plans don't have to be written, but we think the process helps you better organize your thoughts. We are fans of what Alison Jones calls *Exploratory Writing*.[18]

To make it simple, we have listed seven questions below. It's important to take the time to think about these questions, debate them with people you really trust, and iterate them over time. Career plans are not static. They should be dynamic. Most importantly, they should make sense to you.

Question 1

Why do you work? What do you want to get from it or through it?

Question 2

What's important to you about how you go about professional life? What's the most critical to helping you feel authentic and true to your unique needs?

Question 3

What are you good at? What gives you the greatest sense of accomplishment? What aspects of your job inspire you?

Question 4

Can you see a path to getting enough of what you need in (1), (2), and (3) from where you are today? If so, how might you plot a course to achieve that in 12, 24, 60 months from now?

Question 5

If you can't imagine a path from your current job, what are the best alternatives you have open to you today? Can you explore any of them in parallel to what you are currently doing?

Question 6

Who are the five people you can trust to give you complete, unvarnished, honest feedback on your answers to the above questions?

Question 7

Tomorrow, what's the one thing you can do to take a small step toward feeling more satisfied and more fulfilled in your career? What's an easy short-term goal you could set yourself in the next 90 days that might open new doors or create new possibilities for you?

Chapter blink

- 100,000 years of human evolutionary biology have conditioned us to look for role models to emulate and follow.

- It's entirely natural for us in our early careers to measure our progress based on external sources of validation (people pleasing).

- Roughly 5–15 years into our professional lives, purely external forms of validation start to wear thin and lose their appeal.

- It is essential that we don't get stuck in a rut of living professional life based purely on what we think others expect of us – or we may self-destruct!

- The keys to fulfilling, sustainable, professional success are to be self-determined, self-directed, and self-aware.

- The three lessons from the most engaged, fulfilled, energetic, and enjoyable career journeys are:

    Reinvention
    3-Dimensional perspective
    Cause

In three phrases

- MEANS NOT ENDS – Think of your job as a means to an end; know your why.

- BUILD OUT FROM YOUR CORE – Stay tethered to your core identity and don't compromise blindly.

- MAKE THE TR3C – Choose form over function and reinvent yourself frequently.

Alison Edgar MBE
Global motivational speaker and best-selling author

Alison's story is made even more fantastic and inspiring because despite sounding like a movie script, it's entirely real. Her story starts in a council flat in Clydebank, Scotland, conquering dyslexia and academic snobbery, to emerge as the UK's leading sales and entrepreneur coach. Along the way, she has travelled around the world, and battled through a harrowing birth experience, to become an incredible advocate for women battling post-natal depression.

However, it is for her work transforming companies of all shapes and sizes that she is best known – receiving a prestigious MBE in 2020. She was the go-to coach for *Dragon's Den* and Generation Z start-ups and is now a leading motivational speaker for FTSE and Fortune 500 organizations.

Her books, *Secrets of Successful Sales* and *SMASH IT!*, along with her methodologies based on these works, have become the high-performance bibles for modern organizations.[19]

My career story

'My career is far from traditional. In fact, you might say where everyone else was turning right, I always took the left turns!' Alison started her professional journey by landing a job in a local hotel. 'I never dwelt on my career path, never really thought about traditional corporate management tracks; they were a different universe to the one I lived in. What I did know was I wanted to get on, I was ambitious, and I learned things quickly. It was that intuitive sense of how to engage with people, how to communicate important things, that ultimately helped me find my way.'

Alison defied conventional wisdom about how careers are typically built. She took a leap of faith, cashed in an insurance policy, and moved to South Africa. 'It was a massive bet-the-farm moment for me. But I had a sense I would be able to make it work. I knew there was something out there I was destined to do… I just had to be brave enough to find it.'

And what an adventure lay ahead. She proved to be not only a naturally gifted communicator but a superbly skilled entrepreneur. She launched her highly successful sales training company, authored books, and now mentors some of world's most impressive young entrepreneurial talent.

The secret is shared success

'I witnessed first-hand examples of poor business leadership. I never understood it. Companies resistant to change, executives consumed by personal ambitions, the inauthentic preaching that seemed so obviously disingenuous.' Alison has been a staunch advocate for authenticity and being straightforward. 'I've never understood the corporate game playing;

for me the cause, the purpose, the outcomes have always made more sense.

'I think this is where my background and career story helped me. I see how some people can get distracted by leadership and status. The idea that their position and job title somehow gives them a power to direct others. In my world, that doesn't make sense. Tell me about the idea, the outcome, how we can help fix a consequential problem… if you tell me that… well, I guarantee I can help you mobilize an army to assist.'

My career tips

'Well, I think I'd offer two things: (1) Don't believe your doubts… you are much better and more capable than you may think… go out and try. You will surprise yourself. And (2) If you want to inspire others to help you, start by figuring out what you think is important about it. If you think something's important, necessary, then there is a very good chance others will as well.'

Izzy Holder
Co-founder & CEO, Fittle

Izzy Holder's career has seen her make giant leaps from starting out with an MSc in Genetics of Human Disease to the world of banking and investment before co-founding one of the UK's fastest-growing fitness and lifestyle brands.

'I'm often asked how and why I made the transition from genetic research to banking, and then almost as often, why I left the world of finance to start my own business. For me it was a natural series of steps.'

Izzy's gregarious personality couldn't be contained in a lab. She sought more people to collaborate with, learn from, and draw inspiration. 'I think I saw each step along my career journey as just that – stepping stones. Each of my jobs has taught me something new, stripped back another layer. And ultimately, I have been left with this burning desire to put it all into practice, to see how the whole business circle works.'

Together with her co-founder, Izzy has presided over Fittle's impressive growth which included being featured in Selfridges, experiencing huge demand, and receiving glowing coverage in *The Times*, *GQ*, *Sheerluxe*, and *Men's Health*. 'Without doubt, this is by far the most fulfilling and complete professional experience I can imagine. I get to see the whole thing, drive the business forward, fix the problems, and the sense of satisfaction I take is on a different scale to anything I've previously experienced.'

Leadership as a verb not a noun

Along the way, Izzy points out that her concept of what business leadership means has been completely reframed. 'I think like a lot of people, I grew up with the idea that leadership in the professional world was synonymous with a job title, a position. It's quite natural for us to think that way. Many organizations have a sort of up or out hierarchy. The only question was whether when you got the big job you would treat people well or not.'

Izzy reflects on her success with Fittle: 'Leadership is really about responsibility, about getting something important done. About delivering something you have promised... even when the people you need to help you are sometimes like the proverbial "herding of cats". There isn't really any glamour in this, but there is enormous reward. We have developed incredibly mutually beneficial relationships with our virtual team and partners... I feel like we all own and have a stake in what we are doing.

'The thing I'm most often surprised about is speaking with senior executives who lament they don't get to do the interesting and rewarding work anymore. They say they miss the days when they were at the cutting edge of what their businesses do. I find that fascinating. I wouldn't want to swap with them, even for a day.'

Careers tip

'Don't get carried away chasing job titles or status. I think they are traps or at least misunderstood. The old style big corporate hierarchies are in decline anyway. If you look forward, you are far better off starting with something you love to do, something you are good at, and figure out how to put that to work in service of some compelling outcome. If you have a skill you can put to work helping get something done or solving a problem... you'll never be short of professional opportunities.'

Chapter 10

Reframing leadership – from control to shared purpose

In the two previous chapters, we learned a lot about why we play career games and how to break out of this cycle – how to reboot the code in our brain, rewrite our programming to become more self-determined, and develop the ability to build our career and life on our own terms.

This chapter will deep dive into the idea of leadership. The ability to lead and being led is at the core of success. Over generations the idea of leadership has been associated with power and control. The world was built around physical power, superstition, and supernatural anointment. People had less access to information. It was almost impossible to compare and validate outside your immediate surroundings. Power and physical strengths were key to survival. It is important to understand this evolution. In this chapter, we will take you on a journey to explore the history of leadership as a construct, share our experience and thinking, and guide you to think about what it should mean for you. We will talk about four themes:

- The evolution of leadership.
- The emergence of new generational needs.
- The AI effect.
- Adult-level leadership – it's all about choices.

There are some very important distinctions, models, definitions, and contexts that it is essential to understand, particularly regarding how we relate to hierarchy, authority, and peers. Equally, it may be easy to assign all blame for poor outcomes on purely the leadership approach when there is a much more intricate, symbiotic relationship between followers and their leaders. Ultimately, however, it is about realizing that our own actions create dynamic reactions and that in many ways our attitude and behaviour will shape the outcomes we experience.

We will look at different models and will explore and explain how we think about leadership. The headline term for our suggested way of leading is 'adult-level leadership'. But before we explain that let's take a whistle-stop tour of leadership constructs through time.

The evolution and history of leadership

The fascinating thing about leadership is that even back in the 4th century BCE, Greek philosophers spent a lot of time exploring its impact on society, and as a result, what ideal attributes a leader should embody.

In the *Republic Book 1*, Plato stresses that leaders essentially work for others, not themselves.[1] He suggested that the best leaders are wise, virtuous, ruling not for personal gain but for the benefit of all. His student Aristotle went a step further and emphasized the ethical aspects of leadership.[2] He built on Plato's work and introduced the idea that a good leader should have moral values and focus on the common good. The concept of 'servant leadership', made famous much later in the 1970s and 1980s by Robert Greenleaf, was born.[3]

The Renaissance period was hugely influenced and, in many ways, defined by Niccolo Machiavelli's view of the world and leadership.[4] His work promoted the idea that leadership was mostly about power, control, and manipulation. In his key work *The Prince*, he argued that leaders must be shrewd, strategic, and at times ruthless, to maintain control and achieve their goals. His work influenced that concept of Realpolitik and strategic leadership.[5] To this day, you can see many leaders across politics, business, and even woke activism, applying his teachings to how they lead.

With industrialization came a sea change across the globe and philosophers, sociologists, and thinkers started reimaging better ways to lead. Yet structure and hierarchies were still at the core of their thinking. While Max Weber, a German protestant sociologist, argued that charismatic leaders possess extraordinary personal qualities that inspire followers and drive significant change, he still believed in strict hierarchical orders.[6] His work laid the foundation for understanding different types of authority and leadership styles.

Kurt Lewin and James MacGregor Burns were influenced by Weber and advanced his theories. Lewin famously created a framework of the different leadership styles – autocratic, democratic, and laissez faire. [7] Burns took this to the next level and explored the difference between transactional and transformational leadership.[8] His research culminated in his seminal publication *Leadership* (1978), the essence of which was that transforming leadership occurs when leaders engage with followers in such a way that 'leaders and followers' raise one another to higher levels of motivation and morality. Many of the early thinkers on leadership were interested in leadership in the context of society and many of their publications were very theoretical.

Peter Drucker, often referred to as the father of modern management, was influenced by many of the thinkers mentioned above but developed his own perspective and his own school of thought.[9] In our opinion, he was probably the most comprehensive thinker and most public advocate of the idea that management was a key skill to be developed by leaders.

In many ways Drucker was one of the first thinkers to articulate the concepts of decentralization and empowerment. He introduced the concept of knowledge workers, but equally believed that direction setting and monitoring was a vital part of running an organization. He stressed the importance of aligning individual and organizational goals and much of his teaching built the foundation for the research and leadership literature published in the early 2000s. Jim Collins' *Level 5 Leadership* built on Drucker's notions of empowerment and direction setting.[10]

All of these brilliant minds, from Weber to Collins, do, to some extent, offer an idealized picture of business leadership. There is a darker side, a game-playing side, to today's business world – what we have referred to as 'leadership dystopia'. The hijacking of leadership to reframe it in more commoditized, mercenary, and selfish terms. We are not alone in this observation. Professor Gary Hamel has crusaded to point out many businesses have grown their investment in management positions and corporate processes without any demonstrable improvement in performance.[11] And, more colourfully, David Graeber's essay on what he calls BS Jobs provides a more dystopian perspective.[12] Consequently, it seems entirely logical to surmise that something other than pure business need may be driving the explosion of management titles. We suggest a significant factor is 'career game playing'. Proliferation of form over substance.

It is this perspective and dynamic that Shey exhibits in his pursuits to obtain a prized leadership position. For all the pure logic that underpins notions of leadership as a noble pursuit, there is a component of life that has created leadership as the ultimate reward, the prized destination of the most ambitious and ruthless amongst us. We see this as a significant drag or point of friction in existing corporate leadership models. However well intended, they often focus on appointing a person to be the boss of people in the context of a bureaucratic hierarchy.

This simplified 'power introduction' is important to better understand our ideas and thoughts on leadership. We believe that we are at an inflection point that requires rethinking what it should mean to lead in the 21st century. This is amplified by Gen Z coming of age, the implications of years of global shock events from the COVID-19 pandemic, to wars, inflation-pressure, the divisiveness of current political discourse, the climate emergency, and unprecedented technological breakthroughs.

The emergence of the need for greater shared meaning

Every new generation wants to reinvent, to reshape the world, believing that the previous generations don't share their priorities. However, these typical prerogatives of the young are more accentuated and profound for Gen Z.

Gen Z almost represents one-third of the world's population – most of them in countries such as India, Indonesia, and Nigeria. They all are influenced by the desires and lifestyles of western Gen Zers. We live in a polarized world that seems to paradoxically be more connected and yet more parochial than ever. Gen Zers globally, however, share more homogeneous views as a collective than perhaps different generations within the same country. Access to social media across country boundaries, and with a shared pastime of watching TikTok, we face the first generations of digital natives coming of age:

- They don't know a pre-internet time.
- They spent a significant part of their youths interrupted by lockdowns.

- Their young adulthood is defined by the emergence of AI.
- New job categories are emerging and the notion of 9–5 and going to an office is more and more alien to them.
- Prioritizing wellbeing and openness about mental issues has become a key trend among Gen Zers.

Companies, bosses, parents, and educators have not yet fully grasped the significance of these changes and neither has Gen Z themselves. Gen Z is more aware than any previous generation of what they can offer, but they are equally uncompromising on what they expect in return. They are ambitious, have ideals, and often money and material goods are less important than experiences, travel, and building global communities. Many of them, in the western world, are struggling to find career choices that fit their world view.

The most elusive missing ingredient is a sense of purpose. We have made the case elsewhere that this is not unique to Gen Z. While Gen Z may be most vociferous and open about their desire to feel a deeper meaning through their work, this is a much more pervasive challenge that impacts us all. It is in many ways the zeitgeist of our times. Moreover, what we are learning from Gen Z is leadership models that focus on conventional bureaucratic justifications, and power by business title, are respected less and less. This offers us a glimpse into our collective future… the workplace as it will be in the next decade and beyond. The new frontier of work as something greater than just a transactional arrangement. Working, and particularly leading, in this new world will require four things:

- **Direction**: Whether we talk about leading ourselves or leading others, a sense of direction is key. Too often young people are unclear where they want their career journey to go and equally often leaders and parents are unclear how to best provide a sense of direction without imposing decisions and disempowering them.

- **Boundaries**: In our first book, *A Career Carol*, we explained the concept of red lines and the importance of defining them early in life. The same principle applies to leadership; it is important to define the boundaries in which one can operate.

- **Space**: Also defined as autonomy. This is probably the most significant aspect of the new zeitgeist. An increasing expectation, bordering demand, about having space in which to operate. Autonomy and space to operate independently is key to get the best not only out of Gen Z but also out of employees or partners in any professional context.

- **Support**: A very important dimension when working with Gen Z and younger Millennials is that they want and need support. They are open to support, as long as it is provided in a context of equals and not paternalistic. A concept that seems so simple yet is hardly ever sufficiently provided by leaders and organizations. We have developed this skill over the years, and it takes patience and a lot of emotional intelligence (EQ) to provide the right level of support at the right time.

The next generation is hugely talented and motivated but has a much higher need to find purpose in what they do. Considering that this generation will also have far more powerful tools in their hands and more choice and opportunities than any previous generation, it will take a shift in mindset for the organizations they work with for the benefit of society.

The AI effect

Much has been written and published about artificial intelligence over the past few years. It is one of the big technological megatrends and breakthroughs of our time. Predictions vary wildly about timing when AI will be able to deliver which activities and when AI will be more intelligent than humans. However, there seems to be some consensus building around a number of milestones to be achieved over the next 30 years:

- 2026 – songs generated by virtual popstars that can't be recognized as an 'AI-fake'
- 2028 – Top 40 Chart pop song
- 2030 – *New York Times* bestseller written by AI
- 2031 – AI wins a college math competition
- 2033 – AI can completely replace salespeople in some functions
- 2055 – certain surgeries will be done by AI

We have educated ourselves on AI and have gone rather deep to understand what will and will not be possible. Is it a hype or will it change the world? Will people work less and earn more? Can it cure some of the big problems of humankind or will it polarize us even further? The issue is that most people who voice expert opinions on AI have a vested interest, thus it's not so easy to find well-balanced opinions on it.

It seems to be a fact that AI is here to stay; it is a reality that AI and its underpinning technology is not new. It is a fact that if used effectively and responsibly it can be a force for good and help with many of the world's big challenges, such as poverty, supply chain optimization, medical breakthroughs, and climate change. However, in the short term, AI will rather have the opposite effect, at least in the area of climate change as it consumes vast amounts of energy to supply the technology with the power they need to run their training models.

Will it change the world tomorrow and deliver great breakthroughs quickly? Probably not. We are still waiting for the self-driving cars and the passenger drone-taxis that were promised ten years ago. 3D printing has not sorted out our supply chain issues, most of company data is still on spreadsheets and the lauded virtual reality applications are yet to come. However, as with most technological breakthroughs, they are initially overhyped, but we normally underestimate their long-term impact. The internet has been around for a long time, the first email was sent in 1971 and computers first started to digitally share information in 1983, but it was only the fully mobile version that came with the iPhone in 2007 that changed the world and how we communicate and interact.

Our life is unthinkable without the internet on our handheld devices. Shey Sinope's generation will say the same about AI. We have only been using AI for some 18 months, and it has already proven tremendously helpful for research work. Many companies are in the midst of exploring how to replace people with AI, and there will naturally be experiments to eliminate many administrative chores associated with classic forms of management. Budgeting, planning, forecasting, delegation, cascading messages, facilitating collaboration. We can imagine how AI will transform classic middle management jobs over the next 5–10 years.

Moreover, AI will transform the future of ALL work. All professions will be impacted, and some traditional professions will disappear. Career choices will have to be made in this context: agility to constantly adapt, change, and learn will be the superpowers of career success. The role of leaders will radically change. Depending on your perspective, there will either be fewer leaders (in the context of our existing definitions) as the ability for teams to be largely 'self-directed' will become more and more common. In another sense, everyone will become a leader, blurring the traditional lines of work demarcation and compartmentalization. There will still be some special tasks reserved for those capable of demonstrating what we call the 'constructive empathy' necessary to help teams achieve peak performance.

Adult-level leadership – it's all about choices

At the beginning of this chapter, we provided context on why leadership is so important. We laid out the history of leadership and how we have come to doggedly hold on to existing concepts of why organizations are the way they are. There is, however, a compelling case to adapt these concepts for today's generational expectations and technological innovations. We believe we have reached an inflection point. A point where we need to reflect deeply on how we run an organization and how we relate to a small and large organization, but most importantly, how we relate to ourselves.

In our *Groundhog Day* story, Shey finds himself in a typical early 21st-century company structure. There are many layers, lots of hierarchy, and HR has identified a possible solution for every problem. Leaders believe they must be in control; succession planning is structured in a binary win or lose way. 'High Potential' programmes are still the paths to executive glory. Networking and impressing superiors are the easiest way to progress – good story telling and being known is often as, and sometimes more, important than delivering great outcomes.

Shey has perfected this game and yet he is not successful in his ultimate wish. His purpose up to that point was to be accepted to the High Potential programme; the grooming ground for future top executives. He believed further career progress would not only be the path to professional fulfilment but also the key to personal happiness. What hurts even more is that his nemesis, Emi Silva, the smart, yet easy-going colleague is perceived to have more potential.

Shey is devastated that his formulaically detailed, planned strategy didn't work. How could easy-going, admittedly clever, Emi, with no desire to execute power or control, be rated over him ? How could his charming way of asking opened-ended questions be valued more than providing clever answers? How come that improvisation and experimenting counted more than detailed and thought-through plans? Both Shey and Emi made choices. Shey's were based on past success strategies; Emi trusted his instincts and gave himself permission to show up as his authentic self.

What we want to draw out in the final part and fundamental essence of this chapter is the hypothesis that a new form of leadership is required to succeed in the future. This form of leadership is not only relevant for corporations but any organization where accelerated progress in a rapidly changing world is required.

We refer to this way of leading as **Adult-Level Leadership** (ALL), which is basically the best of what has been written about leadership in the past 20 years but hardly ever found in practice. It's also a reference to Thomas Harris and his research on transactional analysis, which was made known in his book *I'm OK – You're OK*.[13] We will not provide a detailed exposition here. Our book is after all designed to be succinct and focused on personal career advice. However, we hold a strong belief that fulfilment in your career is not only linked to *what* and *why* you choose a direction but also *how* you go about it.

We will provide five simple principles in the ALL style that we highly recommend every CEO, leader, or individual think about and consider embracing into their professional approach:

1. **Principle one: Generous listening/hearing** is key – never take more than your proportionate speaking time and stand in the speaker's shoes.

And, just as importantly, engage with what you are hearing.

2. **Principle two: EQ amplifies IQ** – Work on your IQ-EQ-Drive balance. EQ can be developed, allow others to coach you. Give at least one person the permission to be 100% truthful with you – no gloss! Be truthful to yourself. It's great to have a high IQ but think of a high EQ as a multiplier.

3. **Principle three: Guided autonomy** creates winning teams. If people don't understand the direction of the journey, the ultimate goal and the boundaries within which they are not only allowed but are encouraged to operate, you are wasting potential.

4. **Principle four: Don't judge people (including yourself) or things as good or bad**, just evaluate the possibilities ideas can create and appreciate the differences of input. Good and bad are only a function of the system around them. The system might be the problem, not the ideas.

5. **Principle five: It's all about choices and judgement** – Never allow victim mentality to prevail for you personally, your team, or an organization. Life is about choices; we just need to make sure most choices are conscious choices, and we understand the intended and the unintended consequences.

We were very conscious in writing *A Groundhog Career* to show how Shey's life transformed as he began to focus less on obtaining a position of power and control over others and instead came to embrace a purpose... a cause. This is central to how we hold leadership for the 21st century. If you have a strong conviction that something needs to change, that a cause is worth fighting for, or that humanity can be improved by launching a new product… people will willingly, wholeheartedly, and passionately join you. The dynamic of working with people who share a purpose is distinct and radically different to our legacy corporate concepts of Vice Presidents and Managing Directors. Perhaps it sounds idealistic, but it really isn't. It is what makes start-up businesses often so much more effective than long-standing, multi-national businesses. Think about your own preferences: Would you rather work for something that you believe passionately in, something you feel energized by, or wake up to a sinking, depressing feeling each day?

We could write a book about these five principles alone and take it to much more detail, and we probably will someday. At this point we just want to ask the reader to reflect on these principles, and how they could change Shey's groundhog experiences.

Reflection exercises

Thinking exercise #1: Authentic listening

Listening is a core skill that most people haven't mastered. This exercise has three parts.

Part 1: Listening vs speaking time: Over the next week, we ask you to observe and document how much time each person in the meeting you attend, speaks vs listens and whether there are people that take disproportionate speaking time. We suggest that you do this at every meeting you attend; if you choose to do so, you can also do this for private settings. The principle is simple – in order to have a balanced dialogue, every person in the room has the same amount of time to be heard and given time to express themselves.

After the week reflect and draw conclusions of what you observed. Reflect on your own speaking to listening ratio.

Part 2: Quality of listening – automatic vs generous listening: Identify one meeting over the next month that is critical in your professional life. Observe your own reaction and how your brain operates when somebody else talks. Listen to 'the little voice' in the back of your head and become aware of what it says. Don't be surprised if your reaction is either agreeing with what the person says, disagreeing with what the person says, or going for 'lunch' and not listening at all. This is automatic listening and that's most often our default listening setting. Observe, reflect, and document how this 'automatic' listening narrowed your perception and openness to new ideas.

Part 3: Stand in the speaker's shoes and become a generous listener: Identify a few meetings in the upcoming weeks after you have completed Part 2 and practise generous listening. The minute 'the little voice' in the back of your brain tries to take over and whispers 'this is such a bad idea', or 'we have done that before and it didn't work' in response to the speaker, make an intervention, cut the voice off, and listen deeply to the words of the speaker. Try to understand the context and the experience that led the speaker to say what they said. It's not easy and needs practice but it will give you access to a completely different way of thinking.

Generous listening is like learning a language. It needs practice and patience. If not used all the time, it will get rusty. If you master it, you will become a much better person and leader.

Thinking exercise #2: Choices and the power of NO

The concept of choices is simple yet underrated. Many people prefer being a victim and blaming others than take responsibility for their choices and their lives. If you like to be a victim and choose to be a victim, there is no need for you to complete this exercise. If you prefer living your life and career on your own terms, continue.

Truthfully answer the following five questions:

1. When you drank too much and wasted the following Sunday, did you really want to continue drinking or did you just meet your friends' expectations of having a fun night out?
2. When did you last wish you had less weight, and when did you last eat a hamburger with fries?

What is more important to you: the hamburger or a slimmer waistline?

3. When did you last do something you disliked, but your partner convinced you to do it anyway?

4. Have you ever worked in a job or work context you hated for more than six months?

5. How often do you prioritize social media scrolling or web browsing over exercises or getting your work done?

All five scenarios provide choices – many of these choices simply required a NO to avoid bad outcomes. So why would you say YES? We hope that this exercise helps you to discover the power of saying NO.

Chapter blink

- Leadership models and practices that were valid in the previous century are no longer valid; business practices and employee demographics/expectations have moved on.

- Leadership is about leading yourself as much as it is about leading others.

- Influence and good judgement will replace control and power.

- Guided autonomy in the context of shared goals unleashes capability.

- Adult-level leadership is about interactions without hierarchical limitations – substance and content trump seniority.

- The right balance of IQ-EQ-Drive will determine success.

- Constructive EQ will become the new superpower.

- The next ten years will see everyone become a leader and at the same time management ranks in large companies will be decimated.

- Focusing on working toward a shared cause, purpose, and compelling selfless goal is the key to being a successful leader... not a business card or title.

In three phrases

1. AN EXPONENTIAL WORLD – Accelerate your learning.

2. EFFORTLESS IS A MYTH – Attitude is everything, don't render yourself irrelevant.

3. ADULT-LEVEL LEADERSHIP IS THE FUTURE – Work on your IQ-EQ-Drive.

Chapter 11

And finally... a defence of formulas

So, which of Shey's formulas do you think is most accurate? Which one do you think comes closest to capturing the secret of a successful career?

It's a trick question of course. As Shey admits himself, it's probably neither. Life is too dynamic, too complex, too chaotic. Like the proverbial butterfly flapping its wings, creating some infinitesimal disturbance that results in a Barista misspelling your name on a cup of coffee, as you rush to the all-important final day of a promotion assessment centre.

But... it's tempting to live life by rules, guidelines, and heuristics. And, as we hope we have proven in this book, quite a natural component of the human psychological predisposition. We can't go through life analyzing every aspect of every decision until we are absolutely certain we've considered every possible consequence. Imagine being stuck behind the person in line at another coffee shop (coffee is essential to many of our metaphors) who wants to debate whether the organic, fair-trade menu is accurate, demanding the server produce proof and getting a farmer from Costa Rica on the phone to verify they are making a living wage before placing their order. None of us has the patience for that.

The problem is, at least when it comes to our careers, we don't tend to err on the side of over-analysis. We tend to collapse our thinking into the daily routines. We focus on the short term, the next week, day, hour. Whatever we need to do to get to escape the office and go home to watch that amazing Netflix documentary *Inventing Anna*.[1] Think of all the people you know who talk incessantly of how they are so ready to escape work and can't wait for their next vacation. There are people who seem to sleepwalk through much of their working lives, blissfully unaware they are trapped in a repetitive bubble; 48 weeks of boring monotony, interspersed with two weeks somewhere sunny, a Christmas arguing with family over the correct way to play Trivial Pursuits, and the occasional night out drowning sorrows at £8.50 a pint of beer.

Unfair?

Perhaps. Our point is not to criticize or judge what constitutes living your best possible life. We are more interested in nudging, okay perhaps elbowing, people into thinking more deeply about the path they are on. During our lives we will spend on average 90,000 hours 'at work'. Over a third of our lives. Surely how we spend this time deserves some deeper level of analysis and examination than 'I don't care what I do for a living so long as it pays £xx,000.'

Life's too short to play games

In *A Groundhog Career*, we make the case that, particularly when we start our careers, we use forms of game playing to establish ourselves. In our desperation and insecurity to grab hold of a first rung on a career ladder, we persuade ourselves that any tactic, any tool, any shortcut is justified. In some ways, this is our personal 'fake it until we make it' moment. Our insecurities and doubts haunt us and make us feel less capable than those around us. And we tell ourselves, it's just until we get through our job probation period, our first anniversary, or our first promotion.

However, playing career games, particularly when they get us results, can be a bit addictive. Basking in the warm glow of approval and recognition we feel from parents, relatives, and even the envy we witness from friends, fuels the temptation to push the game parameters... playing harder... faster... stretching it a bit further.

And so there is a danger that our game playing ensnares us. That rather than being a tool, it becomes our sole purpose. It happens gradually, insidiously. We become consumed by winning the game, by running ever faster on the metaphorical hamster wheel. Over time, each incremental accolade provides a little less dopamine hit. Every promotion feels slightly less fulfilling than the previous one. This leads to three things: (1) a self-fulfilling, never-ending need to run faster, to play the game harder; (2) an inversion of fulfilment and satisfaction; and (3) becoming trapped in a psychological purgatory where you end up repeating the same day for the rest of your life.

Be yourself... everyone else is taken

The career game is a distraction. An exercise in self-delusion. It keeps us busy focused on external, material forms of desirability and success. When we do this, we are unconsciously (sometimes even consciously) avoiding searching to understand who we really are, what we really enjoy, what makes us unique.

We do this because we have been conditioned to be a 'good child.' That we suspect that who we really are at our core may not be acceptable to the world. It's just a lot easier to choose to be who we think people expect us to be. The trouble with this self-denial/self-repression is that we can end up attempting to navigate an enormous dissidence between the puppet we play for the external world versus the person we believe ourselves to be at our core. However we may wish to deny it, we all hold an idealized version of ourselves that we keep buried inside us. It's like a prized picture of a loved one we keep in a metaphorical locket; the psychological equivalent of a *Dorian Gray* portrait.[2] We ultimately go through life believing everything we do is in service of that inner identity. The trouble is, we have rose-tinted glasses as we excuse ourselves for occasional and cumulated deviations. If we aren't careful, the elastic band that connects the two in our minds can snap. When it does, we can collapse, deflate, as we are forced to re-evaluate who we thought we were. This can cause lasting damage to our egos, and our sense of self-worth.

Generally, about ten years into our professional lives, we naturally come to terms with this dissidence, and we seek to address nagging questions about why we are working, what we are doing it all for. However, we all struggle to reconcile this and many of us (as per the research, half of us), fail to find a satisfactory answer.

This is where we have framed the **TR3C** mnemonic to help illuminate a path. We know what distinguishes those who feel truly engaged, satisfied, fulfilled in their careers from those who don't. We hope we have done something to demystify, explain, describe, and suggest a means to unlock this secret.

From competing to collaborating – redefining leadership

One of the awful consequences of our justification to 'do whatever it takes' to establish ourselves in the professional world is the collateral damage it causes. If we are honest, we can all look back and wince at a memory of some behaviours in our youth. Sometimes it is unwitting but there are too many occasions when we take the 'dog eat dog' approach to the detriment of entirely innocent bystanders. It's made worse by some people around us excusing it and saying, 'don't worry... everyone does that' or 'well... if you'd hesitated... they would have done it to you.'

We reject all of this as self-serving, convenient, conscience disinfectant. The fact is, we can be cruel and thoughtless in pursing business goals, and we should challenge ourselves to justify whether it was necessary, or even productive, in the long run.

We make the case in Shey's story and in our chapter reframing the definition of leadership that we are at our worst when we think of leadership as a status or title to be obtained, and at our best when we use it to describe the formation of a group of people intent on solving a consequential problem. Ultimately, society, humanity, the planet, need more focus on solving collective problems and less emphasis on individual power plays.

As a manifesto for the 21st century, we think leadership as a shared purpose is a much more powerful and accurate way not only to solve huge problems, but also to raise our own sense of fulfilment, energy, satisfaction, and worth. It's the closest thing we've seen to the self-actualization that Maslow theorized.

And... so... what happens to Shey after the final scene?

He gets to live a new day in which to make some new mistakes.

The thing with fairy tales is that they often end with what we think is an unrealistic happy-ever-after byline. Real life isn't like that. Once Shey figured out that his days were resetting every night, he was able to perfect his approach. The conditions were contained and controlled. At the end of the story, he once again faces the same jeopardy of chaotic and unexpected circumstances as the rest of us.

So... he probably finds some new things to get wrong, new roadblocks, and new opportunities. What we like to think, though, is that he is better equipped to handle them. That he has deepened as a human being. He has a new three-dimensional perspective. Moreover, he has escaped the career game trap and is now thinking more clearly about what a fulfilling professional journey might look like on his own terms.

Now, what we are even more intrigued about is what happens between him and Babs the Barista. Sashay or Shantay? These are the sorts of questions that seem even more imponderable than how to live a long, vibrant, fulfilling, professional life.

- The End -

Authors' notes

Shey Sinope and his friends found us in the fall of 2022. We were sitting at our respective computers trying to find a way to tell a cautionary tale about navigating career crises. One Wednesday at 9am Shey's name appeared for the first time. Initially, neither of us paid much attention, but he persisted. He broke down our resistance, regaling us with his satirical monologues about the absurdity that surrounds us. Eventually, we agreed to let him into our story, and within a week, he became the story.

Telling a story is an extraordinary experience. You become an observer and recorder of events. It is as if the story was always there, sitting behind your keyboard, waiting for someone to type the magic first word.

Shey insisted we understand his journey. As we wrote *A Career Carol*, we also listened and recorded what Shey told us happened throughout his 40-year career. Not only the ghostly visits he experienced when he was in his early 20s, but what then happened to him throughout the rest of his life. It was a compelling, and at times, far-fetched story. But there was something about it. Something well intentioned. We found it funny, touching, prophetic, and life-affirming.

How much of this should you believe? There may be a dash of dramatic exaggeration. However, did you know in a survey conducted by Durham University of 181 authors, 61% said they heard their characters speak to them while they wrote? This does not surprise us. Sorry, just a moment, what was that Shey? We know, we know. We'll get to that in the next book.

We hope you enjoy this second instalment of Shey Sinope's journey. We feel privileged he chose us to help him share it. We sincerely hope you enjoy it and at least one person finds the advice helpful.

Acknowledgements

This book wouldn't be possible without all of the people we have both worked with over the years. The people at BP, Reliance Industries, E&Y, Ivoclar, AFS, and the extraordinary entrepreneurial talent we have had the privilege to advise. We have learned so much in working with people in USA, UK, India, UAE, Austria, Lichtenstein, and countless other places. We have attempted to distil and do justice to the enormous wisdom you have shared with us over the past 40 years.

We couldn't have written this book without the training, support, and inspiration from some noteworthy teachers. Dr Oxley would like to thank Jim McNeish, Dr Lockey, Dr Buchanan, Dr Pilbeam, and Dr Vyakarnam. David would like to acknowledge the radical thinking of Shri Mukesh Ambani and Dr Gary Hamel.

A very special thanks is reserved for Roman Schindler, Trisha Conley, Daniel Obst, Rohan Radhakrishnan, Alison Edgar, and Izzy Holder. Spending time with each of you to learn more about your work, careers, accomplishments, and professional lessons has been eye-opening. Your insights bring a wonderful added dimension to this book, and we are grateful for your shared belief in the importance of this project as well as your time and candour.

We are both students of story telling and the rich tradition that dates back to the ancient Greeks of re-telling and updating stories to resonate with new audiences. The movies *A Groundhog Day*, *Palm Springs*, even *Back to the Future*, have left a great legacy on our popular lexicon. The world now widely uses passing oblique and obscure references in general conversation. This a great testament to the power of the underlying stories.

Dr Schuster would like to acknowledge Sue Oxley for being such a supportive and patient force in David's life. David and I acknowledge that our writing exploits are only possible because of the sacrifices and support of others. However, Sue deserves special credit for all that she has done to support us both. Dr Oxley would like to acknowledge and thank Dr Schuster for his patience, encouragement, but mainly all the croissants. The idea, the cause, the problem statement that led to our writing, was Dr Schuster's.

Both Drs Schuster and Oxley would like to thank Alison Jones and her team at Practical Inspiration Publishing. It's been an absolute pleasure and education to work with such professional, talented people.

Special thanks once again go to Andy (Doodles) Baker for his amazing illustrations and to Rachel Moulton for her early encouragement when Shey was still stuck in his dorm room.

A *special dedication* from Dr Schuster to his late mother, Elfriede Schuster. There are so many things to thank her for it may take its own book. I am most grateful that she and my late father Hermann provided me with a good sense of humility and a moral compass that served me so well all my life. Secondly, let me also thank AFS Intercultural Programs for allowing me to study in the US in my mid-teens. It showed me a global, diverse, very different world and set a foundation for everything I subsequently went on to achieve. Thank you, Daniel Obst, for being such a great President and role model for the next Gen. Lastly, big thank you to my swim coach Hannelore Wallisch; she taught me the value of discipline.

A *special dedication* from Dr Oxley to Sue. I can't thank her enough for everything she has made possible in our lives. It has truly been an adventure of a lifetime. Once again to our daughters, Charlotte, Amy, Liz, and Rebecca for their love, support, and unabashed promotion efforts! I may now be able to compete for the second-best author award in our family behind our granddaughter Fynn, who is on her fourth book. I still have so much to learn from her. And thank you to Lane for the volcano shoes; they have become essential during these summer months.

Finally, once again, to my parents Terry and posthumously to Shirley. Thanks for all the encouragement and help with my English essays... I'm finally putting it all together!

Supplementary notes

Introduction

[1] H. Lee, *The Changing Generational Values*, Johns Hopkins University (2022). Available from:https://imagine.jhu.edu/blog/2022/11/17/the-changing-generational-values/

[2] A. Kellett, *The Texas A&M Professor Who Predicted 'The Great Resignation'*, Texas A&M Today (2022). Available from: https://today.tamu.edu/2022/02/11/the-texas-am-professor-who-predicted-the-great-resignation

[3] J. Harter, *In New Workplace, U.S. Employee Engagement Stagnates*, Gallup (2024). Available from: www.gallup.com/workplace/608675/new-workplace-employee-engagement-stagnates.aspx

[4] *The UK's workforce is one of the most dissatisfied in Europe*, People Management (22 June 2023). Available from: www.peoplemanagement.co.uk/article/1827408/uks-workforce-one-dissatisfied-europe

[5] J. M. Horowitz & K. Parker, *How Americans View Their Jobs*, Pew Research Center (2023). Available from: www.pewresearch.org/social-trends/2023/03/30/how-americans-view-their-jobs/

[6] A. H. Maslow, *Toward a Psychology of Being*, Princeton, NJ, Van Nostrand (1962).

Chapter 2

[1] S. Sinek, *Leaders Eat Last*, London, Portfolio (2014).

Chapter 5

[1] L. L. Lehtinen, *The haunting artifice of fake villages around the world*, CNN article (2018). Available from: www.cnn.com/style/article/potemkin-village-gregor-sailer/index.html

Chapter 6

[1] S. Jeffries, *War in Ukraine, death of the Queen, Elon Musk… why are Nostradamus's 'predictions' still winning converts?* The Guardian Article (2022). Available from: www.theguardian.com/books/2022/oct/10/why-nostradamus-predictions-are-still-winning-converts

[2] B. O'Connell & M. Adams, *What Are Angel Investors?* Forbes Advisor (2022). Available from: www.forbes.com/advisor/investing/what-are-angel-investors/

Chapter 7

[1] Plato, *Plato's The Republic*, New York, Books, Inc. (1943).

[2] M. Heidegger, (1889–1976), *Basic Writings: from Being and Time (1927) to the Task of Thinking (1964)*, New York, Harper & Row (1976).

[3] W. James, *The Principles of Psychology*, New York, H. Holt (1918).

[4] A. H. Maslow, *Toward a Psychology of Being*, Princeton, NJ, Van Nostrand (1962).

[5] F. Herzberg, B. Mausner & B. Snyderman, *The Motivation to Work* (2nd ed.), New York, John Wiley & Sons (1959).

Chapter 8

[1] S. McLeod, *Oedipus Complex: Sigmund Freud Mother Theory*, Simply Psychology (2024). Available from: www.simplypsychology.org/oedipal-complex.html

[2] B. E. Turvey & J. L. Freeman, *Recently Effect*, Encyclopedia of Human Behavior (2nd ed.) (2012). Available from: www.sciencedirect.com/topics/psychology/recency-effect

[3] B. Frimodig, *Heuristics: Definition, Examples, and How They Work* (2023). Available from: www.simplypsychology.org/what-is-a-heuristic.html

[4] W. B. Cannon, *Bodily Changes in Pain, Hunger, Fear and Rage*, New York, Appleton & Co (1915).

[5] S. Freud, *The Ego and the Id*, New York, W.W. Norton & Co (1961).

[6] P. S. Peters, *The Chimp Paradox*, London, Vermilion (2012).

[7] D. Kahneman, *Thinking, Fast and Slow*, New York, Farrar, Straus and Giroux (2011).

[8] M. Gupta & A. Sharma, *Fear of missing out: A brief overview of origin, theoretical underpinnings and relationship with mental health*, World Journal of Clinical Cases (2021). Available from: www.ncbi.nlm.nih.gov/pmc/articles/PMC8283615/

[9] S. McLeod, *Stanley Milgram Shock Experiment*, Simply Psychology (2023). Available from: www.simplypsychology.org/milgram.html; S. McLeod, Solomon Asch Conformity Line Experiment Study, Simply Psychology (2023). Available from: www.simplypsychology. org/asch-conformity.html; S. F. Brosnan & F. B. M. de Waal, Fair refusal by capuchin monkeys, Nature (2004). Available from: www.nature.com/articles/428140b

[10] D. Kahneman, *Thinking, Fast and Slow*. New York, Farrar, Straus and Giroux (2011).

[11] B. E. Ellis, *American Psycho: A Novel*, New York, Vintage Books (1991).

[12] A. H. Maslow, *Toward a Psychology of Being*, Princeton, NJ, Van Nostrand (1962).

[13] F. Herzberg, B. Mausner & B. Snyderman, *The Motivation to Work* (2nd ed.), New York, John Wiley & Sons (1959).

14 R. A. Easterlin, L. A. McVey, M. Switek & J. S. Zweig, *The Happiness-Income Paradox Revisited*, National Academy of Science (2010).

15 H. I. Lebow & L. Lawrenz, *Are Empaths Real? Here's What Science Says,* PyschCentral (2023). Available from: https://psychcentral.com/blog/empaths-are-real

Chapter 9

1 The State of American Jobs, *How Americans view their jobs*. Pew Research Center (2016). Available from: www.pewresearch.org/social-trends/2016/10/06/3-how-americans-view-their-jobs/

2 L. Wachowski & L. Wachowski, *The Matrix*, Warner Bros (1999).

3 P. Guyer & R.-P. Hortsmann, *Idealism*, Stanford Encyclopedia of Philosophy (2021). Available from: https://plato.stanford.edu/entries/idealism/

4 S. Kelly, *The Matrix: Are we living in a simulation?* Science Focus (2022). Available from: www.sciencefocus.com/future-technology/the-matrix-simulation

5 E. Goffman, (1922–1982), *The Presentation of Self in Everyday Life*, Garden City, NY, Doubleday (1959).

6 J. Abram, Donald Woods Winnicott, Institute of Psychoanalysis (2015). Available from: https://psychoanalysis.org.uk/our-authors-and-theorists/donald-woods-winnicott

7 V. Satir, *Your Many Faces: The First Step to Being Loved* (NEW EDITION), Berkeley, CA, Ten Speed Press (2009).

8 B. E. Ellis, *American Psycho: A Novel*, New York, Vintage Books, (1991).

9 L. Festinger & J. M. Carlsmith, *Cognitive Consequences of Forced Compliance*, Journal of Abnormal and Social Psychology, 58, 203–211 (1991).

10 A. Sessa, *What Happens When Charismatic CEOs Crash?* Rice Business School (2022). Available from: https://business.rice.edu/wisdom/features/charismatic-founder-ceos-behavior

11 S. Carlin, *The True Story Behind Netflix's Inventing Anna*, Time (2022). Available from: https://time.com/6147088/inventing-anna-true-story/

12 **TR3C** is our mnemonic – a play on the word TREK. See Drs Schuster & Oxley for more.

13 R. Frost, 'The Road Not Taken', *An Introduction to American Poetry*, edited by Lisa Swank, London, Viking Press (2015).

14 B. Sylvester, *Fact Check: Did Oscar Wilde say, 'be yourself, everyone else is already taken'?* Checkyourfact (2019). Available from: https://checkyourfact.com/2019/08/27/fact-check-oscar-wilde-be-yourself-everyone-already-taken/

15 C. Moore, *Introduction: Socrates and the Precept 'Know Thyself'*, Cambridge, Cambridge University Press (2015). Available from: www.cambridge.org/core/books/abs/socrates-and-selfknowledge/introduction-socrates-and-the-precept-know-yourself/FCFA794C8AAD6FDF463866F13DA90F62

[16] A. Gillan, *Not the retiring type: meet the people still working in their 70s, 80s, and 90s,* The Guardian (2015). Available from: www.theguardian.com/lifeandstyle/2015/aug/01/still-working-aged-in-70s-80s-90s

[17] D. J. Levitin, *Successful Aging: A Neuroscientist Explores the Power and Potential of Our Lives,* New York, Penguin Publishing Group (2020).

[18] A. Jones, *Exploratory Writing: Everyday Magic for Life and Work,* Practical Inspiration Publishing (2022).

[19] A. Edgar, *SMASH IT* (2021) and *Secret of Successful Sales* (2018), St Albans, Panoma Press. Visit Alison's website for more info at: www.alisonedgar.com/author

Chapter 10

[1] Plato, *Plato's The Republic,* New York: Books, Inc. (1943).

[2] R. Kraut, *Aristotle's Ethics,* Stanford University Encyclopedia of Philosophy (2022). Available from: https://plato.stanford.edu/entries/aristotle-ethics/

[3] R. Greenleaf, *Servant Leadership: A Journey into the Nature of Legitimate Power and Greatness* (25th anniversary ed.), edited by L. C. Spears, Mahwah, N.J., Paulist Press (2002).

[4] N. Machiavelli, (1469–1527), *The Prince,* New York, Penguin Books (1981).

[5] J. Bew, *Realpolitik: A History,* Oxford, Oxford University Press (2015).

[6] M. Weber, *The Protestant Ethic and the Spirit of Capitalism,* Abingdon, Routledge (2001).

[7] C. Nickerson, *Leadership Styles and Frameworks You Should Know,* Simply Psychology (2024). Available from: www.simplypsychology.org/leadership-styles.html#Lewins-Leadership-Styles

[8] J. M. Burns, *Transforming Leadership: A New Pursuit of Happiness,* New York, Grove Press (2003).

[9] Peter F. Drucker, (1909–2005), *Classic Drucker: Essential Wisdom of Peter Drucker from the Pages of Harvard Business Review,* Boston, MA, Harvard Business Review Book (2006).

[10] J. Collins, *Good to Great,* New York, Random House Business Books (2001).

[11] G. Hamel & M. Zanini, *Humanocracy: Creating Organizations as Amazing as the People Inside Them,* Boston, MA, Harvard Business Press (2020).

[12] D. Graeber, *Bullshit Jobs: A Theory,* London, Penguin (2018).

[13] I. T. A. Harris, *I'm ok – You're ok: A Practical Guide to Transactional Analysis,* New York, Harper & Row (1969).

Chapter 11

[1] *Inventing Anna,* created by Shonda Rhimes, Netflix (2022). Available from: www.netflix.com/title/81008305

[2] O. Wilde, (1854–1900), *The Picture of Dorian Gray.* London; New York, Penguin (2003).

Index

www.ingramcontent.com/pod-product-compliance
Lightning Source LLC
Jackson TN
JSHW021227090225
78679JS00003B/5